THE

PURPOSE-
DRIVEN

Social Entrepreneur

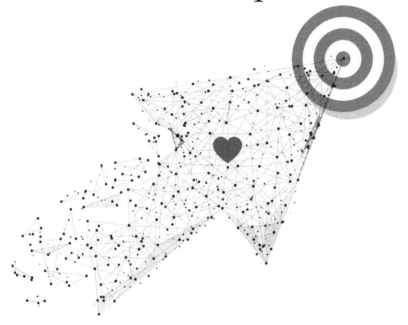

THE

PURPOSE-
DRIVEN
Social Entrepreneur

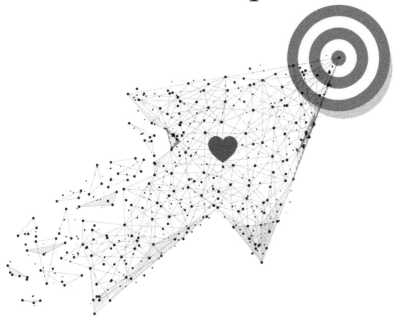

KARIM ABOUELNAGA

Indigo River Publishing

Editors: Jackson Haynes and Regina Cornell
Design: Robin Vuchnich

Indigo River Publishing
3 West Garden Street, Ste. 718
Pensacola, FL 32502
www.indigoriverpublishing.com

Ordering Information:
Quantity sales: Special discounts are available on quantity purchases by corporations, associations, and others. For details, contact the publisher at the address above.

Orders by US trade bookstores and wholesalers: Please contact the publisher at the address above.

Printed in the United States of America

Library of Congress Control Number: 2019930200

ISBN: 978-1-948080-69-9

First Edition

With Indigo River Publishing, you can always expect great books, strong voices, and meaningful messages. Most importantly, you'll always find…words worth reading.

Table of Contents

PREFACE

This book was written by someone who exudes passion, for people who at some point in their lives have been passionate about something, and for anyone who wants to make decisions with more intention and purpose. My journey as a social entrepreneur, an eighteen-year-old founder, an executive director of a nonprofit, and a CEO of a public benefit corporation has heavily influenced this book. This book sets out to help you answer the questions: How do you know when you've found a passion that is worth pursuing? How do you live a life of purpose without losing your passion? How do you start something meaningful?

I have experienced the highs and the lows of being a social entrepreneur. There have been moments along my journey that have forced me to question the significance of my work, whether I was on the right path, and whether I could sustain the work I was doing with the financial, emotional, and psychological toll it takes on me daily.

My purpose is to improve public education to ensure that all kids have an equal chance at fulfilling their life's ambitions. My goal is that everyone who finishes this book will at some point in the near future speak their purpose into existence with the same level of conviction that I have in mine. Only then can we create a world of more engaged, intentional people whose collective actions inspire the billions of people on this planet to do more good.

INTRODUCTION

I spent my freshman year of college at the City University of New York's Baruch College. Just before that, my older brother and I had graduated from Long Island City High School in the same year. Because our parents came from little means and were immigrants in the United States, my siblings and I wound up attending some of New York City's most struggling public schools. Our high school had well over 4,000 students when I was a freshman, with roughly 1,400 in my freshman class, but just under 530 in my graduating class. Of the kids who graduated, only a fifth were estimated to be college-ready. While the societal expectations were never truly that high, it took me several years to fully understand why.

My first semester at Baruch had wrapped up and I had received a 4.0 GPA. Excited by the news, I reached out to a few adults that I had started to develop relationships with, many of whom I had met through a nonprofit I participated in when I was in high school called

Rewarding Achievement (REACH). Encouraged by their responses, I took a leap of faith and decided I was going to transfer colleges.

I realized that I had gone about my college application process all wrong the first time around. Instead of applying to a school that was well regarded for the major I wanted to pursue, I should have applied to the school or university that was the best school I could possibly get into—you know, just in case I decided to change majors or pursue something else, which I eventually wound up doing.

After a visit to Cornell University in February of 2010, I decided I was going to apply to their School of Hotel Administration. My senior year of high school I was rejected from Massachusetts Institute of Technology (MIT). It was the only other school besides Baruch that I put a meaningful amount of effort into getting into. I visited the campus and went on an alumni interview. Unfortunately, or fortunately, it did not work out.

Nonetheless, the rejection from MIT bruised my ego, and I never anticipated I would apply to another elite school. Until I visited Cornell. At the time, I was working at an aquatic center when my boss had a friend who was going up to visit the university. She suggested that I spend the weekend with her and check out the campus and see what it had to offer. Initially, I didn't jump on the opportunity, but eventually decided to take advantage of it and made the trip. Besides, I had a childhood friend there whom I could visit and spend time with if I really was not enjoying the trip.

When we finally got to Cornell on a bitter-cold day in February, I asked my childhood friend Nick to meet up. I got to see his studio and meet some of his friends, all of whom were normal-looking and -acting people. For some weird reason, after I got rejected by MIT, I thought all of the kids who were at these top colleges and universities were brainiacs of some sort. Since I was not a brainiac, I figured that not getting into MIT was for the better. Nick's friends may have been brainiacs, but I could not tell in the couple of hours I had known them. In fact, the topic of advanced placement (AP) courses and tests taken in high school came up, and Nick's friends openly shared how they had scored poorly on some of the same ones that I had gotten threes and fours on. (AP tests are scored on a scale of one to five, with one being the lowest and five being the highest, and if you score a three, you usually get college credit.) That discovery led me to believe that I might actually fit in on one of these campuses, and that maybe I should consider applying to transfer.

When I asked Nick and his friends what school I should apply to, they initially suggested I apply for the applied economics and management program in the College of Agriculture and Life Sciences. I laughingly said I did not want to be a farmer. That was when they suggested the School of Hotel Administration. It was sort of like a business school, but they focused on hotels and restaurants. Oh, and by the way, they said the kids there were pretty cool.

I got back after the long weekend, and I could not stop thinking about getting into Cornell and the School of Hotel Administration. I started thinking about my personal statement, and I started looking into scholarships. It was like senior year of high school all over again, except this time I was a lot more excited. I felt like I had found the perfect school for myself. Surprisingly, this was also where my journey of purpose really started. While I do believe there is an element of choice about what to focus your life on, I also recognize that there is an element of serendipity, where you find yourself engaged in something that means so much to you.

One of the scholarships I ran across was funded by the United Negro College Fund and Coca-Cola. In 2009, McKinsey & Company had just published a report on the impact of the achievement gap in America's schools. The report was a huge deal in education and showed that the gaps between blacks and whites were costing the economy over $300 billion in GDP each year, which was the economic equivalent of a permanent national recession. The gaps between kids who were rich and kids who were poor had a negative economic impact that was almost twice that. One of the report's conclusions was that we could avoid the economic downturns that existed if we were able to close the gaps in achievement between black and white kids and rich and poor kids. This was especially pertinent in 2009 because of the housing bubble that led to one of the biggest recessions since the dot-com bubble burst and the Great Depression. The significance of the report was compounded by the United States Census's findings that the demographics in America were changing much more quickly than previously anticipated. In fact, where the disparities were widest, among white and nonwhite children, nonwhite children were expected to make up more than 50 percent of the school-aged population by 2023. Recent data has shown that we have reached that point in 2015.

The scholarship offered a $10,000 award to any student who could come up with a solution for the achievement gap that involved corporate intervention. I still remember how puzzled I was originally. I did not know what the achievement gap was or how corporations functioned. I had never heard anyone around me reference the disparities in achievement between my friends and me and some other kids somewhere else as an achievement gap before. And none of my parents or immediate family members worked for a corporation. As such, I was limited in my understanding of what a company could do to solve this problem that I believed I was completely unfamiliar with. Nonetheless, I wanted $10,000 to transfer to Cornell. I figured I could learn the things I did not know with a little bit of research. After all, there was a significant amount of money on the line.

In my quest to understand corporations and the achievement gap, I discovered how wrong I was initially. I knew the achievement gap and the disparities that existed much more intimately than I had anticipated. My entire childhood could be summed up by achievement gaps. I found myself enamored with what I was learning, then I found myself consumed, and shortly after I was frustrated.

For months, as I prepared my application for Cornell, I researched the inequalities in education. I tried to further understand the problems in education. I did not just care about the proposal; I wanted to solve the problem. How could such a well-defined and simply articulated problem be so hard to address? That was just the beginning. As I started to work with my advisor, I began to understand why the solutions to this challenge of the achievement gap had alluded practitioners for so long. An element of the problems was believed to be genetic, and thus inherited. An element of the problems was believed to be environmental, and thus could be changed, but are complicated to change in a society that incentivized those who were motivated to take on more and do more.

After months of work, I submitted a solution that I believed had some merit. The research I was running across showed that the more engaged parents were in their children's learning, the better their academic outcomes were. There was this trickle-down effect. While I loved my mother dearly, she rarely if ever tried to help me with my homework, largely because she herself did not understand what I was doing in school.

I started to think back to my own schooling, and I remembered the concept of fractions being introduced to me as early as fourth grade, and then it was repeated every year after. Maybe the essential years of parental involvement are early on. It seemed that if kids had a solid foundation, then they could rely on it for the years to come.

I proposed a compulsory learning program for parents in low-income neighborhoods who had children under the age of eleven, right around the transition between elementary school and middle school. My advisor at the time questioned the viability of another social welfare program at the time where our country was undergoing a major financial restructuring to keep up with the recession. I remember pushing back and saying there would be no additional funds necessary to put such a program together; we would just tweak the already existing incentives. Growing up in a low-income household, I knew the various types of support that our family relied on: EBT benefit card, Social Security income, Medicaid, food stamps, etc. Instead of adding more funds, I thought, what if we instead made it an obligatory requirement for the parents receiving the assistance with children under the age of eleven to dedicate some time, an hour or two a week, to learn the material they needed to help their kids succeed? I believed the simple act of the parents' trying to learn would inspire the kids to work a little harder and mimic their parents. We could test the parents monthly or quarterly, and if they did well, then we could boost their welfare slightly. If they did not engage, we could shock or suspend their aid as an incentive to work. Besides, their child's education or lack of education did not just impact them; it took a toll on society. This was their social obligation.

A week after I submitted this proposal, which I thought was brilliant, I was assured how horrible an idea it was. I asked one of my friend's parents if they were asked to partake in such a program what it would mean. They laughed. Fortunately or unfortunately, the money is controlled by the adults. He mentioned that if money were taken away from him, then the money would just be taken away from his kids. It did not affect him as much. He would still prioritize the things that he wanted. It was a sobering moment for me after the months of hard work on this idea and proposal.

I never won the scholarship or the award. I did not even receive an honorable mention. Rightfully so. I ignored a critical part of the instructions. I never figured out how to weave in corporations to help address the achievement gap. But the frustration and burning desire to solve this problem stayed with me. I carried it in my heart, in my mind, and in my pocket, where the $10,000 check I never received would have been held until I arrived in Ithaca to start my sophomore year at Cornell.

PART 1: *PURPOSE*

How do you find your purpose? How did you find your purpose? Those are two of the most frequently asked questions I get after delivering a talk or visiting a university. It may be that I speak to a selective audience of people who care more about figuring out how to make their lives count, or maybe we're entering a period of time where people are questioning what the purpose of money is and whether there's meaning behind it.

The proliferation of media and social media has raised awareness of human pain and suffering globally. Sharing information and research on disparities and inequality has never been easier. With eight people in the world now controlling just as much wealth as the 4 billion people who make up the poorest half of the world (according to Oxfam), we now know that money alone will not solve the large-scale problems, like hunger, sex trafficking, and racism.

In a world with so many social problems and challenges (or opportunities if you're entrepreneurial), how do you know which one to dedicate your life to solving? And how do you know this is your purpose?

In order to unpack those questions, you need to understand the difference between passion and purpose. Passions are the simple things in life that we enjoy doing, things that encompass everything from a deep burning desire to make sure everyone is treated equally to an activity or a hobby like riding your bike or painting. While the vast majority of the things you are passionate about will never materialize into your life's purpose or be purpose-driven work, I do not believe you can run into purpose without first engaging in your passions. Ultimately, it is passion that will fuel your purpose.

This first section takes you through the questions that mattered to me, the ones I believe people engaged in their purpose can answer with conviction.

Chapter One

Starting from Scratch

Question 1: Why Is This Important?

"We don't accomplish anything in this world alone . . . and whatever happens is the result of the whole tapestry of one's life and all the weavings of individual threads from one to another that creates something."
—Sandra Day O'Connor

This is the first of my six purpose-finding or purpose-framing questions. The first question helps you understand if what you are spending your time trying to solve or address is even worthwhile. Being able to articulate why the topic or the issue you care about is an important one also ensures that you will be able to find other people in the world who care about this problem—because no one ever solves anything worthwhile single-handedly.

The most important piece about framing your issue is to make it big enough to pass what I call the "requiring help test." When I was first starting Practice Makes Perfect, I did not ask people to come and help me put together a summer program for thirty fourth-grade students in my neighborhood in Long Island City, Queens. Anyone who knew me then would have probably looked at me and said, "Karim, you are smart and hardworking, and I am sure you would be good without my help." And they would have been absolutely right if that was all I was trying to do! Instead, I reached out to them and I framed the problem I was trying to address in a much larger context. I went around telling people that I wanted to narrow the achievement gap.

From McKinsey's 2009 report on the impact of the achievement gap on America's schools, I found that the achievement gap was costing our economy upwards of $300 billion each year, which was the economic equivalent of a permanent national recession. When I was fundraising or trying to get others to volunteer their time or even commit themselves to joining my team, I would lead by telling them that the problem I was trying to address directly impacted our economy. It was not just about educational equity or running a summer program. We had an opportunity to do something that could help improve our economy.

This passed the requiring help test. The problem was so big and so important that someone who heard me say I wanted to address it would react by thinking, "Karim, you are smart and hardworking, and I am sure you are going to need my help to be able to make a dent in solving this problem." This encourages others who care about this problem or some facet of it to be compelled to support you in your journey.

Of course, in your first couple of years you may not even be significant enough to make any sort of impact on the problem. In my case, I was always thinking about ways to increase our impact. I had my eyes set on the bigger social issue of the achievement gap and creating a more equitable society. If I was ever going to make any headway in addressing those social ailments, then I would have to get people to see why this problem was so large and important while simultaneously doing what I was capable of to get the initiative going.

Most really big, successful things start really small. The purpose of starting small is to test your initial hypothesis and assumptions. Sometimes you are limited to starting really small because you do not have a lot of resources, or maybe you are like me and you are in college without access to a lot of money. In fact, starting small allows you to get the kinks out and get some initial results that could get more people interested and excited about your work. Your job as the leader of the initiative is to inspire others to join you and help grow your solution to the identified issue.

If you are a social entrepreneur or someone who is constantly trying to raise money or lobbying for a cause, the first question after you establish yourself as credible is inevitably "why is this important?" There are millions of causes and organizations out there. Everything from poverty to homelessness to sex trafficking to immigration reform to new problems that arise daily because of the internet is an issue. As the space becomes more and more crowded, the question "why is the problem or the cause you are spending your life working on important?" matters even more.

Chapter Two

Personal Connection

Question 2: Why Is This Important To You?

"If it is important to you, you will find a way. If not, you will find an excuse."
—Author unknown

I was at Echoing Green's All Fellows Retreat in October of 2017 when I attended a reception that was cosponsored by the Campaign for Black Male Achievement. The speaker shared a story about how one day she noticed that there were ants starting to infiltrate her garden, so she started laying stones down to keep them out and throw them off. After she did that, something very fascinating happened. Instead of marching in their straight line like they had been, the ants created new routes. They started to go over, under, and around the rocks to get to where they were going in the garden. She closed by letting the group know that if they were going to succeed as social entrepreneurs, they were going to have to be a lot like the garden ants.

I would like to take this concept a step further and broaden it to include everyone who is in search of their purpose. Whether you are just starting to find your purpose or are toying with the idea, something will inevitably get in your way. There will be an obstacle, a setback, someone who is trying to scare you, social pressure, or a friend who is advising you to do otherwise. The burden to go over, under, or around falls on you. The garden ant expends more energy having to get around the rock now than it had to before the rocks were placed there, but it is necessary in order to succeed.

This brings me to the second purpose-finding or purpose-framing question that I reflected on: Why is this important to you? When you have purpose, you have a reason. That reason is what propels you. It pushes you through the obstacles and the setbacks that will inevitably come your way. And it is not just any reason; this is a reason that matters to you. It is personal.

While the last chapter was all about framing the problem as being important to everyone so you can mobilize other people to support you in your journey, this chapter is all about what it takes to mobilize yourself. This chapter is about framing your problem and what you are doing in a way that is consistent with what you care about. At the end of the day, if you are not inspired or moved by the reason, then it does not matter.

As I started to learn more about the achievement gap and the disparities in education, I grew incredibly frustrated. I kept thinking about how there were so many people out there who knew about the inequalities that had existed in education for so many decades, but very little progress was being made. I read statistics like first-generation college students graduate at a rate of 11 percent over six years. College was advertised as four years, yet this statistic had to be put at six years or else it might not have broken double digits. I learned that 80 percent of the kids graduating from New York City public schools who attended community colleges had to take at least one remedial class. That meant they were paying to take classes in college that were free for them to take and pass in high school. I started to wonder why they were being allowed out of high school without meeting all of the requirements they needed for college.

The energy and excitement I received when I thought about the inequality was nothing short of incredibly moving. That was the explosive energy I needed to get to and through Cornell like I did.

When I finally decided it was time to start Practice Makes Perfect, I was moved by a sense of purpose. At the time, I believed it was only a passion. But in hindsight, I know it was a sense of purpose, and by the time I got to my senior year of college, it had become a sense of moral obligation. I knew why the work was important to me. If I had made one wrong turn at any moment in my path or if I had not had the amazing support of the mentors and the nonprofit organizations that stepped into my life to make sure I was on track to succeeding, I could just as easily have become a negative statistic.

The premise under which we founded Practice Makes Perfect was that all children, regardless of race or socioeconomic status, have equal potential to compete intellectually in our society. It means that no matter where you are born, what your skin color is, or how much money you have in your pocket, you have the opportunity to unlock and achieve your full potential. Much like I was doing.

As I continued to build Practice Makes Perfect, it was increasingly obvious to me that I was engaged in my purpose. Much like the kids who are at an educational disadvantage, I was raised by a single mother, I grew up in a low-income neighborhood in a household where English was not my primary language, my family relied on government assistance for food and health care, I was a first-generation college student because no one in my family had gone to college in the United States (let alone, my mother only finished high school in Egypt and my father dropped out of high school in Egypt), and I identified as Black or African American. I could just as easily have been the kid who never made it past the educational disadvantage barrier as I was the kid who made it out and started to defy the odds. That is why this work was important to me. I wanted to make sure that I created something that allowed kids growing up just like me the opportunity to overcome these barriers.

Far too often, I meet people who claim to be walking in their purpose, without an understanding of why they personally care about the work. You need to understand why this job or this organization or this cause you are committing yourself to is important to you. Without that full understanding, it will be incredibly hard to act like a garden ant when the rock is put in your path to deter you from moving forward.

Chapter Three

SELF-EVALUATION

QUESTION 3: WHY ARE YOU THE RIGHT PERSON TO BE DOING THIS WORK?

"There is a saying that every nice piece of work needs the right person in the right place at the right time."
—Benoit Mandelbrot

At any given moment, I have dozens of approaches or solutions for problems and policies that affect my neighborhood and our country. Some of these solutions are probably ridiculous ideas. Others might have some potential. Unfortunately, none of them matter if I do not have any credibility in the area in which I am proposing the solution. How excited would you be to get culinary lessons from your doctor? Driving lessons from your lawyer? Tax advice from your barber? I am sure there are a few prime examples of barbers who are certified accountants, lawyers who manage driving schools, and doctors who are culinary aficionados. But that is not the norm. More often than not, you go to your lawyer for legal advice, your doctor for medical advice, and your barber for advice on how to style and maintain your hair.

The final piece of purpose-finding that guided my own reflection was whether or not I was the right person to be carrying out my work to reform public education. Because if I was not the right person, it would not matter if I found an important problem that others identified with or that it was a problem that was personal to me. If I could not convince myself or other people that I was the right person to be engaged in my work, then it would not matter, because I would never be able to garner the support and the resources to address the issue I was so passionate about.

So let us talk about credibility and things that matter to your audience. One element—and the one I believe is the most powerful—is personal experience with the problem or the solution. Another element that is noteworthy is formal training on addressing the problem or education on the solution. The last element that I believe adds credibility is general experience/wisdom in a related field or area that is similar to the one you are trying to pursue.

Too often, I find people who believe they are engaged in their purpose after they think of a problem or work that they would like to do. They often have the initial passion but lack a reason why it's personal. Purpose is passion sustained over long periods of time. We may have an initial inkling that we care about and are willing to devote ourselves to only to find out after a few days, a couple of weeks, or a handful of months that this is not how we want to spend our time or our efforts.

One of the things that I found most really successful entrepreneurs have in common is that they intimately understood the problems they were facing. In many regards, Jeff Bezos wanted to make books more accessible online, Larry Page and Sergey Brin wanted to sort information so it would be easier to find, and Bill Gates wanted to make software that would increase the functionality of a computer. In all of those cases, they started to address problems that they had experience grappling with personally. When they spoke about the solutions they were designing, they already had a greater understanding of the problems they were facing than the average person who was also facing that same exact problem. But this is purpose on a big scale.

Separate from the entrepreneurs who faced the problems personally, there are people who do not start companies or businesses, but instead join them because they are aligned with their missions and they believe in their solutions. I have seen people who were denied social services as children rise up and join social services organizations when they became adults. Similarly, I have seen people who received social services rise up and join social services organizations. It is not uncommon to find people who love to travel and experience cultures join companies that allow them to spread their joy for travel and experience with other cultures to help people find destinations to visit and learn from. I have met lawyers who, after receiving a particular type of counsel when they were children or being denied that counsel, pursue law with the intent of providing that counsel for others. And, of course, there are those doctors who have seen a loved one pass too early and became inspired to help others not have to face the same outcome. They wake up every single day moved by something bigger than themselves, but most importantly, they understand the complexity of the problem they are trying to address.

There are other ways to build the credibility that you need to be engaged in purpose-driven work besides intimately experiencing the problem that you are trying to address. The broadest area of credibility is the one where you have experience solving the problem in an unrelated area, but the skills you learned in the process are presumably the ones you need to be meaningfully engaged in the work you are interested in. I like to think about fields that are general but largely applicable to almost every industry. For example, if you have spent ten-plus years hiring college students for their first jobs to work for a pharmaceuticals company and now you apply to work for a financial services company hiring college students for their first jobs, odds are you will have a lot of credibility pursuing that other opportunity. The same can be said for people who are working in marketing, sales, management, and finance. Having experience in those functional areas will provide you with credibility if you decide to continue to work in those same areas, regardless of the industry. Of course, there will be nuances and jargon to understand to help make you successful. But the point here is credibility, and it can be transferable across industries.

As I thought carefully about taking the leap after college to work on Practice Makes Perfect full time, I knew people would judge me based on how passionate I was. I also knew that people would judge me based on whether or not they believed I could actually do this work. I was twenty-one years old and needed to raise hundreds of thousands of dollars from lots of different people, so it was important that people believe in me. Not only was I fortunate enough to have experienced the problems firsthand and intimately understand the problem but I also had a host of business experience from working in my father's store as a kid, interning in financial services while I was in college, and studying business while I was in school. My initial reservations were quelled when I started to think about how I had the skills and the knowledge I ultimately needed to be successful.

Chapter Four

Timing Is Everything

"Without urgency, desire loses its value."
—Jim Rohn

Once you have the answers to the three original questions you reflected on (why is this important, why is this important to me, and why am I the right person to be doing this), you have won a third of the purpose-driven battle. The next two pieces that you need to discover and reflect on for yourself involve inspiration and then timing.

As it pertains to inspiration, it is not enough to come up with responses that sound good. No one has ever committed their entire life or even a portion of their life to something because it sounded good. The reality is that it also has to feel good. You need to feel like what you are doing is the right thing because it feels right. Maya Angelou has a famous quote that says, "People will forget what you said . . . but people will never forget how you made them feel." You need to help other people feel like this is the right thing to do.

At this point, if you have the clarity you need when you think about the three questions and they are enough to inspire you—so much so that you cannot wait to finish getting through this book so you can get started on that job transition, volunteering for the organization in your neighborhood or starting your own organization—then you are at a good point. If you are not, take another moment, pause for a little and continue to reflect on these three questions in order:

1. **Why is this important?**

2. **Why is this important to me?**

3. **Why am I the right person to be doing this?**

By now, you have clarity and you can, at least, subjectively say that you are inspired by the reflection you have done. The last piece of the puzzle in your purpose-finding journey is to think about the timing. Sometimes you will find things that are important, they mean something to you, and you believe in your heart of hearts that you are the right person to be engaged with them, but the timing is not right. In fact, this is something that would have been great for you to have done five or ten years ago or that would be great five or ten years from now. The easiest way to modify these questions and find out is to add a bit of urgency to them by adding some variation of time sensitivity. Be careful not to jump to these questions directly and to only reflect on these three after you have answered the first three.

4. **Why is this important right now?**

5. **Why is this important to me right now?**

6. **Why am I the right person to be doing this right now?**

We all have had that friend who has had a dream that they never pursued because the timing was not right for them. They started raising a family, they did not have enough money, or the forces of the universe were simply working against them. Those things are real—okay, maybe not the last one, but the other things are real—and they matter. Ignoring where you are in this moment and failing to have the self-awareness that is necessary to successfully reflect on those questions could be to your detriment. I remember thinking about the first three questions and coming to a point where I knew the work I was doing mattered to society. The achievement gap impacted the economy, so it was relevant to other people. Then I got to a point where I understood why my work in education was meaningful to me. I was the first one in my family to graduate from college, and I had people and organizations that helped me get to that point. And I finally understood that I was meant to be doing this work because of my unique perspective in the education space.

For some strange reason, that clarity was not enough. I had people say, "Karim, that is great, and I believe in you, but you should come back to this when you are older and have more money or more experience." And, of course, being the stubborn millennial that I was, I would ignore them. But you can only ignore people for so long before you start to doubt yourself and everything you believe in. By the time I got the same set of advice for the thirtieth time, I became discouraged. I started to think that maybe everyone was right. This work is meaningful and important and I should be engaged in it, but just not at this moment. The moment you start to believe that, it actually comes true. It was not until I had the realization that my reflection was missing a little more intentionality that I overcame the discouragement. It is why I always say the reflection is not complete with those three questions until they are expanded to include the three questions that I outlined with the time-sensitivity variation.

Why is this important right now? There are thousands of issues and jobs out there that you could engage with: homelessness, malaria,

Zika, poverty, etc. The majority of people want to focus their time and efforts on things that are important in this moment. Of course it is important for every child to have an opportunity at an equal education, but with so many other persistent problems, something else needs to exist to move people to act on this issue right now, in this very moment.

When I thought about why the work I was doing was so important right now, I reflected on the statistic, published by the United States Census in 2010, that said by 2023 minority children would comprise more than 50 percent of the school-aged population. That stat created the urgency around the work that I needed to justify to myself and to others that this problem needed to be addressed sooner rather than later. Minority children were the ones who were most likely to attend disadvantaged schools and were most likely to fall victim to the achievement gap. If we did not work to start reversing the inequality and close the gaps in achievement, the negative impact on the economy would only continue to be compounded. If we acted today, we could at least make an effort to rewrite the future.

When you think about why the work you want to pursue or engage in is particularly important or timely for you in this moment, make sure you reflect on why it did not feel like that yesterday and why you cannot see its being as important for you to pursue a few years from now. Timing is everything.

Why am I the right person to be doing this right now? Despite all of my efforts to educate my friends and mentors about what I was involved with and how it was revolutionizing summer education, they still saw Practice Makes Perfect as a tutoring company or an after-school program. If that was what they saw it as, then I needed to reflect on that question with that context in mind. Why was I the right person to be running an after-school program or a tutoring company right now? I had never run an after-school or a tutoring company before. There were people out there who had run these types of companies for years before. If you are looking to transition from one industry to another, ask yourself what indicators or qualities you possess that make you believe that you can be the best person for that particular opportunity right now.

When I thought about why I was the right person to be doing this work right now, I kept thinking about how much freedom I had in that very moment. I was ready to graduate from college with zero dollars in debt. I was young and had little to almost no familial obligations. I had the fortune of hearing older entrepreneurs come to my classes and encourage the students to go into entrepreneurship early. They made it clear that the risk is very high. You have to want and be ready to go all-in. And that is much easier to do when you are right out of college without kids or a family than it is ten or fifteen years later.

There could not have been a better time for me. I only discovered that my work with Practice Makes Perfect was more a part of my purpose after years of believing it was my passion. I got to the right point in my life where it made sense to reflect on these questions with my purpose-driven work already in my mind. It also gives me hope, and helps me to believe that all of us are already engaged in work or in something that is waiting for us to claim it as our purpose. We just have not done the reflection yet.

I made these six questions the foundation of my reflection and the ones I have advised people to reflect on before they begin any purpose-driven work, because they are the most common questions that you will hear from your friends, your family, your potential supporters, and beyond.

Chapter Five

DEFY THE ODDS

"It's the repetition of affirmations that leads to belief. And once that belief becomes a deep conviction, things begin to happen."
—Muhammad Ali

One of the funny things about purpose is that everyone is looking for it, all the time, whether they are consciously looking or subconsciously looking. When someone around them says they have discovered their purpose or are going to engage in purpose-driven work, their natural instinct is to react in disbelief. They default to questioning how someone else could have found their purpose while they are still looking and have probably made very little progress. They may even believe that life has no purpose and while they are on Earth they just need to live. So when someone in their presence finds their purpose, it puts to question their own beliefs.

That person may very well have been you or someone you know. It may have been what inspired you to pick up this book. Now, instead of asking those questions of others once they have found their purposes, you have the tools to ask them of yourself.

Going back to my initial point, what matters more than the responses to the questions that you reflect on is whether or not you believe in the responses to the questions. You know in your heart of hearts that the response is true beyond a reasonable doubt. The events and the moments in your life that you are pointing to that have lead you to this very point were not orchestrated by chance or mere coincidence.

I have had far too many moments that have grounded me in my purpose after coming to this realization. After I graduated from college, I was running my organization full time. Within a month, I wrote a hand-written letter to a billionaire hedge fund manager who had supported nonprofits and programs I was a part of when I was in high school. With no expectation of a response, I received an email a month later to set up lunch. The lunch got delayed and rescheduled twice before we finally met in person. By the time we were ready to meet, I was two weeks short of missing payroll. Of course, I had been directed to the hedge fund manager's family foundation weeks before I came in for lunch, but they had respectfully denied my funding request. At the time, I asked them for $70,000 to support our team for the upcoming year. By the time the lunch rolled around, I viewed it more as a formality than as a request for funds.

Somehow, the conversation strayed in the direction of my funding request. I told him I had been denied and encouraged to apply later. Within moments, he reversed the decision and approved a grant request for $100,000. The amount was more than we had asked for, but exactly what we needed to give me faith that I was indeed engaged in my purpose.

My entire life has been set up in an odds-defying fashion. The odds of traversing the ladder of social mobility at the rate that I have were slim. The odds of graduating from my high school and being college-ready were slim. The odds of my attending and graduating from an elite college were slim. The odds that I would work on Wall Street were slim. The odds that I would be so connected to the hundreds of people who would one day work with me on my mission to improve our public education system were slim.

The best tool to evaluate the thoughtfulness of the responses to your purpose-driven questions is to reduce the likelihood that something could have happened just because there was a high probability that it would happen. Work to understand why it uniquely happened to you. Another thing you can do is ask yourself, *what are the odds?* If the odds are little to none, as they were most of the time in my case, then you are well on your way to engaging in work and in life with more intentionality and purpose.

Ultimately, what you are trying to do is have enough conviction in your reflection that you believe it beyond a reasonable doubt. People will question you and your ability to identify and engage in your purpose the moment you share that you believe this is the work you are meant to be doing. The more conviction you have in your responses, the more committed you will be to your work. You will be more unwavering in your aim to achieve your purpose because you know that this is your reason for being on Earth at this very moment, at this very time.

Chapter Six

Purpose in Action

"The two most important days in your life are the day you were born and the day you find out why."
—Mark Twain

In 2016, *Forbes* granted me my own column and gave me the latitude to cover anything I wanted. I chose to cover people who were living in their purposes. I profiled over a dozen individuals from whom we could all learn something. They wake up with a sense of urgency and a desire to improve the world. They all believe their lives and their work are about something much bigger than themselves. The following are three of their stories.

How This 27-Year-Old Filmmaker Is Helping People with Disabilities Own Their Narratives

Reid Davenport, 27, was born with cerebral palsy and has dedicated his life to giving people like him a voice in today's narrative. "For a while, I watched news and documentaries that portrayed people with disabilities as inspirational tropes, passive bystanders, or villains.

I was none of the above. I had a story and was living with a disability," said Davenport. According to a 2011 United Nations report, there are over a billion people in the world living with a disability; almost 200 million experience very significant difficulties.

"The increasing prevalence of social media and the need for the broader public to understand that people with disabilities are not all inspirational, passive, or villains makes me believe that people with disabilities can take back the narrative by sharing their own stories through video and streaming on platforms like Facebook," says Davenport. Now there are over 2 billion monthly active Facebook users, of which one billion are daily active users.

Davenport started making films about people with disabilities almost seven years ago, after he was discouraged from studying abroad in Europe because of its lack of wheelchair accessibility. "Instead of quenching my desire to explore Europe, I applied for the Luther Rice Collaborative Fellowship to travel to western Europe and document my experience and the lack of physical accessibility for people with disabilities," Davenport said. The trip led to one of Davenport's most well-regarded documentaries, a 28-minute film titled *Wheelchair Diaries: One Step Up* that received the award for Best Short Documentary at the 2013 Awareness Film Festival.

"I have lived with a physical disability all of my life, and I learn more about myself when I make films. Rather than attempting to cure society's hesitancy toward disabilities and disabled people, I turn to filmmaking, which allows me to appreciate my own struggles unlike anything else," said Davenport. He's gone on to produce four other short documentaries that explore the perspective of people with disabilities and has received a handful of other awards, including the Artistic Visions Award at the 2016 Big Sky Documentary Festival.

In 2016, Davenport took his work one step further when he cofounded Through My Lens, which is an organization that works with schools and community centers to teach students with disabilities how to collaboratively make films. "I think other young people with disabilities who have gone through identity issues or internalized frustration could potentially benefit by expressing themselves through video. I've experienced the catharsis of recognizing and sharing my struggles through video," Davenport said. He hopes that his work will lead to more narratives from the perspectives of people with disabilities. "In a media that is riddled with the disabled human-interest stories that strengthen the taboo of disability, firsthand perspectives—whether they're feature films or Facebook live events—will show what it's really like to be disabled in today's society," said Davenport.

How One Digital Marketer's Inspiring Story Amassed 1.7M Followers

Nathan Allen Pirtle believes his purpose is to help leaders understand how to use social media to connect authentically. "First it was radio, then it was television, and now it is social media," Pirtle says. Per the Pew Research Center, as of January, 70 percent of Americans use social media for entertainment, connection, and news.

"Social media helped one person rise from the bottom of the Republican rankings to President of the United States," said Pirtle. With eight months left to go until the general election, President Trump had an estimated $2 billion in free media coverage. This allowed Trump to spend about half of what Clinton spent on her campaign—$238.9 million compared to $450.6 million. Pirtle believes, "if we teach the right people how to use social media, they can be the leaders of tomorrow."

In 2014, Pirtle founded a digital media company called Work with the Coach to help leaders connect authentically with their fans and consumers. "Nobody wants to be sold to on social media," Pirtle says. "When you engage with your fans in a genuine way, the fans will organically spark business." His start is a testament to just that.

Pirtle landed Wyclef Jean, one of his more recent celebrity clients, through a cold tweet.

And though it might seem like Pirtle was always at the top, his life's journey tells otherwise. Pirtle was born in East St. Louis and raised in Decatur, IL. The cities rank as being safer than 3 percent of other cities and 12 percent of other cities in the US, respectively. After years of disenchantment with school, Pirtle dropped out when he made it to tenth grade. The next few years were marked by instability. He did what he needed to do to fit in and avoid standing out. Before he knew it, he was arrested for an armed robbery and was looking at a prison sentence of fifteen years to life. Pirtle caught a lucky break and got off with six years of probation and only one year in jail.

In 2013 Pirtle's father passed away, and it marked a turning point in his life. "I packed up my things, moved out to Los Angeles, and picked up jobs at a call center and at Coffee Bean while I was starting my digital media company," he said. He was convinced that social media was the wave of the future. The territory is also very familiar. Just a decade ago, Pirtle used to manage an artist's brand and his own page on Myspace. "It's a gift I was always good at. When I started my company, I did it using a twenty-nine-dollar app," said Pirtle.

Earlier this year Nielson published a study that showed adults eighteen and over spend, on average, over five hours per week on social media, with the heaviest users spending over three hours per day. "Social media is one of the biggest opportunities companies have to connect directly to consumers," the report stated. Pirtle echoed this same sentiment.

"Most digital media companies advise people on how to build their brands, but they don't have people engaging or following them on their own platforms. Digital marketing and social media should be about letting people into your life and helping them feel like family," he said. Today, Pirtle has 1.7M followers on Twitter. His company has several notable celebrity clients and has worked with Nicki Minaj, Lil Wayne, Wyclef Jean, and Paula Abdul. He's been credited for worldwide trends and each month reaches over 100M between his Twitter following and client list.

His following and what he calls "family base" didn't really start to grow until he owned his story. Pirtle shared, "At first I was afraid to tell my story because I believed that people would judge me. One day I just put it all out there. I accepted that I wasn't perfect and I will never be perfect. Once I came to terms with my mistakes and the things I did wrong, people started to respond positively to it. They were able to relate to me on another level because we all have skeletons in our closets, we all have secrets, and we've all done things we wish we didn't do." The rise of social media has provided us with an opportunity to augment our reach and our presence.

This work for Pirtle goes beyond his day-to-day. He believes that minorities need more role models who aren't just athletes and entertainers. He believes that if black boys pursued coding, medicine, and business with the same vigor they do becoming a rapper or an athlete, then we'd have more black men doctors, programmers, and entrepreneurs. "There aren't that many minorities in digital media. I want my story to inspire. I want to be that one piece of hope when it feels like there is no hope," Pirtle concluded.

HOW ONE MARINE BIOLOGIST IS WORKING TO SAVE THE GIANT CLAM

About ten years ago, Mei Lin Neo, 31, was tasked with reproducing an offspring of giant clams. What was originally supposed to be just another science experiment, where she would take the larvae of the offspring to examine for a few weeks, has now defined Neo's lifelong purpose to save the giant clam. "I faced multiple failures in trying to rear the giant clams to age, but I couldn't give up. During my work, these microscopic larvae did not give up; they showed me what it meant to fight for their survival and want to be alive," said Neo.

Today Neo is the world's leading scientist on the giant clam, as measured by publications in the field. "When I finally succeeded, I felt immensely gratified to 'give new life' to these miniature giant clams. This became a constant reminder for me as to why I go to work daily, knowing that I can help make a difference and develop solutions to help save a species," said Neo. At the time, Neo was just starting to discover that giant clams were on track to extinction because of the rapid over-harvesting that took place in the 1960s and again in the 1980s.

According to Neo, the case to conserve the giant calm is a no-brainer, especially as it pertains to its role in protecting coral reefs. The National Oceanic and Atmospheric Administration estimates that the tourism industry is boosted by $30 billion globally because of the coral ecosystem. Giant clams are known to make their shells out of calcium carbonate, the same material hard corals use for their skeletons, which allows their shell material to become a part of the reef framework.

Also overlooked is the role giant clams play as greenhouses for algae. The most important living things on our planet are algae, because they produce more oxygen through photosynthesis than any other living thing. Algae need sunlight to grow, but too much is harmful, so giant clams, which have tiny iridescent cells inside their mantles, create a perfect balance. Not to mention, giant clams also serve as shelters for fish, small shrimps, and crabs.

"Most definitely, there have been other predecessors who attempted this work before, and I see myself continuing their legacy. I don't think I'm better than anyone else, but I'm different in how I am obsessively interested in the giant clams and my utmost determination to work out smarter conservation solutions," said Neo. According to Neo, as the marine environment continues to be disrupted by human pollution and apathy, we need to take a multidisciplinary approach to conserving giant clams. "Conserving giant clams may very well extend towards the conservation of reefs and their inhabitants," said Neo.

Part ii: *Mindset*

One of the most revered entrepreneurs of all time, Henry Ford, summed it up best when he said, "Whether you think you can, or can't, you're usually right." Being an entrepreneur, succeeding in life, accomplishing goals, or realizing your biggest dreams comes down to your mindset. If you can tame your thoughts and control your mind, you can shape your outcomes. I spend a decent amount of time on mindfulness meditation because it allows me to work on focusing my thoughts and my energy.

Being an entrepreneur is not easy. The mental toll is large, and having the right expectations is important. In a 2013 *Inc.* article titled "The Psychological Price of Entrepreneurship," the author reveals that many entrepreneurs harbor one common secret demon: "Before they made it big, they struggled through moments of near-debilitating anxiety and despair—times when it seemed everything might crumble."

Unfortunately, there is no easy way around the mental battle. One of the things that helped me early on was imagining that the entrepreneurial journey was essentially a compressed sine graph (that graph that they showed you in math and physics that you never imagined you'd ever hear referenced again) that was tilted slightly upwards.

Starting a company is much like being on a roller coaster, with all of the ups and downs and twists and turns. It feels like one percent of your time you're on top of the world and another one percent of your time you're in the bottom of the bottom. The remaining 98 percent of the time you're either on your way up or on your way down. Now, I try to stay humble when I'm at the top so that I have the strength and the endurance to pull through when I feel like I'm at the bottom.

The next set of chapters will walk you through my reflections and my mindset at the beginning and beyond on my journey building and running my company.

Chapter Seven

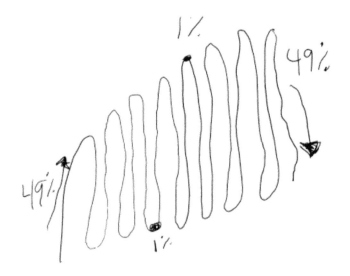

MAN IN THE MIRROR

"Do not go where the path may lead, go instead where there is no path and leave a trail."
—Ralph Waldo Emerson

Every great book on purpose—and I am certain there are many—should start with a disclaimer, one that goes something along the lines of: "This book may or may not help you find your purpose. In fact, if you believe you have found your purpose after reading this book, please send the credits my way. If you are still lost in your search for purpose, that is okay. If you did not find your purpose, please do not give up. And lastly, if you believed you had found your purpose but later discovered that it was not and later find a better way to help others discover their purpose, just remember that all sales are final."

When it comes to purpose and meaning, we all want the same thing. We want to know that we were put on this Earth for some reason. We want something that is going to motivate us to get out of bed in the morning and do something.

When it comes to discovering your purpose, there is a good chance you will be wrong. There is also a good chance you may be right, and right multiple times because you may have multiple purposes. One person who comes to mind when I think of the notion of multiple purposes is George H. W. Bush. While he found purpose in serving his country as the forty-first president of the United States, raising his son who later became the forty-third president of the United States is just as purpose-worthy. I am in no way saying that your kids have to be the president of the United States for it to count as purpose-worthy, but I am saying that raising a family or guiding the next generation of our youth is purposeful. Many teachers and youth advocacy workers have that privilege every single day.

Knowing how high the stakes are when it comes to filling the longing desire to know what your purpose is in life, I thought it would be especially fitting to share with you one of the most sobering truths about success. I have seen shades of it throughout my childhood, my adulthood, and in the lives of other people. I have read memoirs about it and have heard many notable people reiterate it. That is, when you are rich and successful and happy, people will be drawn to you. When you are poor, unsuccessful and depressed, the people who were drawn to you before will not be by your side. This is true regardless of where you grew up or the social circles you maintain.

Let's start with one of the most valuable insights that I learned along my journey to the purpose-driven work and the purpose-driven life I lead. Keep the learnings in this chapter front and center as you reflect through the rest of my perspective.

It was my senior year of college, and I would soon graduate from Cornell University's School of Hotel Administration. I had a full-time offer to work in Black Rock's fixed-income portfolio management group following my successful summer internship. The offer was for a yearly salary of $70,000 plus a one-time signing bonus of $10,000. If I turned the offer down, I would be able to dedicate myself full time to working on Practice Makes Perfect. That came with zero dollars and a zero-dollar signing bonus. I would later discover that it would come with a lot of agony, lost friendships, broken promises, and demanding sacrifices on my behalf.

Like most anxious college graduates, I wanted to make the best decision possible. After all, I would not be able to bounce back from a big failure as fast as some of my peers with more extensive family connections could. On one side, I was told that the time after you graduate from college is the best time in your life to take risks because you have the least amount of responsibility. On the other hand, I was told that it would be really dumb to turn down an offer where I could make that much money at a company that was so well respected at a time when my family had so little. The pressure caused paralysis, and I tried for as long as possible not to make a decision. If I'd had the perspective I have today, I would have made the decision so much faster.

When we find ourselves in moments where we have to make difficult decisions like that, the most responsible thing to do is turn to someone we trust and get advice. In some cases, we even find ourselves deferring to an older person and asking them to make the decision for us. That sounds good and peachy until you realize it is your life. The only person who can make the most informed decisions about the things occurring in your life is you.

At the time I was graduating, I had a couple of mentors tell me I was crazy to even consider my company as an option. If I turned down my Black Rock offer, I would never get that kind of opportunity again. It got to a point where I had mentors who were so passionate about the advice they were giving that it was not really advice anymore. They really just wanted me to do what they thought was best.

I knew that if I took their advice, I might be able to continue to go to them until I stopped doing what they told me to do. But what good would it be if the advice was the wrong advice anyway? If I did not take their advice, they might feel like they had wasted their time sharing their perspectives. They might go as far as severing ties.

Nonetheless, something did not feel right about taking the advice that would lead me to Black Rock right out of college. I started to believe that my mentors who were telling me to take the $80,000 offer to support my family did not fully appreciate the importance of the work I was carrying out or how I truly felt about my work. It sounds silly in hindsight that I was the one who was upset with them for looking out for what they believed was in the best interest of my family.

However, it was in that moment that I asked myself: *In 10 years, success or failure, will I be happy?* The answer to that question really worked me up when I thought through the worst-case scenario, which was my standing in front of the mirror feeling like a failure and knowing I had let someone else make the decision for me.

One sign of a great leader is someone who takes credit for their failures and owns up to their mistakes. In that moment, I realized that the first person I needed to be accountable to was myself. What the actual decision was going to be did not matter as much as who made the decision. The most important thing was knowing that I was the one who made the decision, because standing in front of that mirror alone in ten years as an unhappy failure who had made the final decision would feel better than standing in front of that mirror alone in ten years as an unhappy failure who had lived someone else's life or listened to someone else about how I should live my life.

The same is true for you as you read this book. Avoid the temptation to use my experiences as advice for your life or for finding your purpose. Instead, take it in as perspective. Understand that what I have done is one way. Doing it the same exact way may lead to a different outcome. What matters is not the outcome, but that it is the right outcome for you.

I ultimately made the decision to turn down my Black Rock offer and to continue building my company. I have not had and do not foresee any regrets. Almost a year later, I was fortunate enough to find a mentor who would help me grow Practice Makes Perfect. His name was Jacob Lief, and he had founded Ubuntu Pathways during his senior year of college at the University of Pennsylvania almost twenty years earlier. During one of our first meetings, he gave me a spin on the "man in the mirror" advice when he told me, "You know your business better than anyone else." Jake made it very clear that he would never tell me what decision I should make; that was my job as the CEO, because I knew my business better than anyone else ever could.

You know your life better than anyone else; do not let someone less experienced with your life make the decisions that impact and influence how you live. Instead, gather perspective and reflect. There are so many factors to consider when making a decision that we do not always have the time or the words to describe. In every decision, we need to consider the relationships impacted, the emotions involved, the potential outcomes and which we desire less than others, the historical decisions made, and the level of urgency. To adequately convey these things to someone else would take hours before they could give you the best decision. Instead, use the time you have with a mentor to learn from what they know best: their decisions and the outcomes of those decisions. Then internalize the parts that are most applicable to you to make the final decision.

Today, I avoid people who advise me on what to do—and you should too. Instead, I find myself gravitating toward individuals who share their own experiences and insights, which allows me to pull parallels and make my own decisions. That is how everyone should live their lives: owning their own decisions. Focus on the outcomes, internalize the perspective, reflect on your own life, and own your final decisions.

Chapter Eight

LIVE ON YOUR CLOCK

"Live your life by a compass, not a clock."
—Stephen Covey

By the time I graduated from college and people found out what I was up to with Practice Makes Perfect, I started to get requests to speak, mentor, and answer questions from people all around the world. Time after time, I would hear people say, "I don't even remember what I was doing at your age, but I definitely was not changing the world." People would comment on my young age, they would mention how impressed they were with me, some would flatter me, and others would talk about me like I was a Martian because of what I had accomplished. Time and time again, people would compare me to their lazy, unmotivated, undriven children. It was gratifying at first, but quickly became too much. I became annoyed that so many parents were judging their children based on a side-by-side comparison to me.

In 2015 I got invited to give two small graduation speeches, one to the seniors graduating from the School of Hotel Administration at Cornell, where I got my degree, and the other to the kids graduating from the second year of their fellowship in a nonprofit called America Needs You, which I participated in when I was a sophomore and junior in college. By the time I got to the graduation speeches, I was so tired and fed up with comparisons that I made that the theme of my talk, not only because it was obnoxious to consistently have people compared to me but because we all find our purpose at different points in our lives. At any given moment, we might be in the middle of a life event or experiencing something that is going to eventually give us the clarity we have been looking for to move forward and act on our purpose. Here's the talk with some minor tweaks so it is reader-friendly:

> *Let's talk about time. When people asked me about my theme for the talk and I said it was going to be about time, the first thing they did was laugh. If there is anything I am really good at doing, it is making sure I never have time, because I have used it all—every single minute of every single day. Then they laugh because they think that I am going to talk to you all about time management. And, of course, they know with all of the things I take on that I am probably not the best person to talk to you all about time management. So I won't.*

> *And just for the record, I actually never planned on talking about time management, because I don't believe that there is such a thing as time management or a time management expert. If there were, I would definitely hire them.*

> *See, the truth is we can't manage time. We can manage our lives, but definitely not time. No matter what we do, the clock will always continue to tick. Isn't that cool?*

No matter what we do, the clock will always continue to tick.

Time is such an obscure concept.

If you're here today, you probably know that there is never enough time. And you're probably hoping that my speech doesn't run too long. Because how ironic would it be if the person speaking about time didn't understand the value of it?

Well, I do, so I'll make my points quickly. Because this day and this time is all about you.

When you graduate from the America Needs You program today, the one thing you need to understand is that everyone has an internal clock. And everyone's internal clock is wired very differently. Some of your clocks will tick for a very long time, and others not so long. All of our clocks started ticking at different times, and they will likely stop ticking at different times too.

Now you're probably thinking, why is this twenty-three-year-old alum talking to you all about such a depressing topic on such a happy day? It's because four years ago, or thirty-five thousand sixty-three hours ago, I was in your place.

And it actually isn't that depressing. I want you all to enjoy the same success I have been blessed enough to see since then. I want to prevent you all from making the one mistake that so many people our age do, and that is sitting there and drawing your life's path based on the people sitting next to you.

Do not take jobs or make personal decisions based on what the people sitting next to you are doing. Be your own person. Define a fulfilling life for yourself and chase it. Because fulfillment does not come from a job, from volunteering, or from working at a not-for-profit. Fulfillment comes from within. Fulfillment comes from understanding what you enjoy doing and what you do not enjoy doing and then increasing the amount of time you spend on the things you enjoy doing and reducing the amount of time you spend on the things you do not enjoy doing.

The only thing worse than taking jobs or making personal life decisions based on what the people next to you are doing is comparing yourself to what the average person your age is doing. You wind up running through life and spending your precious time seeing where you stack up. You lose sight of the fact that we all have one life and that we were all put on this Earth for a reason. We can spend our time searching for that reason or we can define that reason. We can spend our time planning what we want our meaningful life to look like or copying what others have done.

Try to avoid being a duplicate at all costs. If you do not have a goal or a purpose for your life today, I want you to leave this room knowing that your purpose or your goal is to make an impact, to make a dent in our world.

Stay away from trying to compare yourself to others. Even more importantly, do not sit there and compare your life to the average person or the average life. If you do that, you will be average. The average person gives back. The average person does not make a dent. And if you were average, you would not be here today.

You are all capable of so much more than average. In fact, you should all skew the average. Do not let the average define you. Each and every one of you has the capacity and the bandwidth to effect real change and make a dent in our world. The reality is that your clock may run much longer or much shorter than the person's sitting next to you—and that is okay.

It is not how many days or hours we have; it is what we do with those minutes and seconds that count.

So do not waste the time that you do have thinking about the average path or your friend's path. Instead, define your path.

I used my time in America Needs You to build and sustain meaningful relationships with my mentors, the volunteers, and their friends. They opened my eyes to the possibilities. And to this very day, they have continued to support me.

Two of them are in this room here today: Lev and Rob. And from each of them I learned something different. From Rob I learned that things do not just happen; you have to make them happen. In his words to me in an email we exchanged in 2011, he said, "Hustle never sleeps." If you have had a chance to spend some time with Rob, you will know that it is a very "Rob" thing to say.

And from Lev I learned that you need to follow your gut and that at the end of the day, the most important person you have to answer to . . . is yourself, so do not live someone else's life.

Since my America Needs You experience, I have gone on to graduate in the top 10 percent of my class at Cornell, raised almost $2 million to advance summer education for economically disadvantaged youth who grew up like me, and directly influenced the lives of over five hundred children through Practice Makes Perfect.

Lev, Rob, and I have a few things in common: we were all raised on modest means, have loving mothers, and have made a conscious decision to dedicate a portion of our lives to developing others, whether that be through America Needs You, Practice Makes Perfect, or Hunter College.

You all have the capacity and the bandwidth to effect real change. Each and every one of you can make a huge dent in our world. And we need more of them.

So again, do not sit there comparing yourself to what the average is or to what other people are doing. Your clock may run much longer or shorter than the person's sitting next to you—and that is okay. Your one real obligation in this world is to be you. Be the most authentic and genuine version of you.

So, when you graduate today . . . go ahead and compare averages . . . I dare you.

Thank you and God bless you all.

The first disservice is when people compare themselves to you and their kids to you. The second disservice is when you start to compare yourself to others. And the final disservice is when you begin to compare yourself to the average. The only thing you need to be concerned with is your time. Do yourself that service and start to frame your thinking through the lens of your time.

Chapter Nine

MARRY IMPACT, NOT IDEAS

"Without execution, 'vision' is just another word for hallucination."
—Mark V. Hurd

All of our purpose should be rooted in making an impact. What is the alternative? A great idea. Far too often, we are enamored by a great idea. We start to visualize what it could look like when it comes to fruition. Only after we actually attempt to execute it do we start to realize the imperfections and flaws in "the great idea." When that moment arises, some of us will sit there and see the beauty in the imperfections. While I, too, believe that we should not disregard an idea or an approach because of one initial setback, I do believe that we should not get strung up on any one particular idea or approach, especially as entrepreneurs or social entrepreneurs.

Iterate, pilot, iterate, pilot, iterate, pilot—every great entrepreneur and innovator knows that this is the process to creating something of true value. In this context, *iterate* means to collect feedback and improve your existing service or product, and *pilot* means to sell or try out again. It is very easy to imagine the most successful entrepreneurs as having a monopoly on the right answer. But that would mean Bill Gates woke up one morning and imagined Windows 8, Steve Jobs was in his garage when he imagined the iPhone 6, and Mark Zuckerberg was strolling down the streets of Palo Alto one morning when he imagined the most recent iteration of Facebook. However, we know that it did not happen that way for any of them.

A few years ago, I had this realization that the most successful entrepreneurs and problem solvers do not start with the desired solutions or approaches in mind; they start with the desired impact or the outcome. Then they start to reverse engineer the rest of the process. They have an idea of how to start achieving that desired impact, whether it is a nicely designed phone or a social network, but they do not have the final product fully sketched out. And that is a good thing. It allows them to be fluid with their product and service.

When I visit classrooms, I lead mini thought exercises with students to get them to truly understand what I mean when I talk about starting with the desired impact. I ask kids to imagine they are in New York and would like to get to Washington, D.C. How many different ways could I get there? There are numerous possibilities: I could walk, I could bike, I could take the train, I could fly, I could drive a car, I could take a bus, or I could carpool with a group of other people. In this case, the desired impact or the outcome is getting me to Washington, D.C. Taking the train or the bus or walking are different solutions or approaches. When there are no time or financial constraints, all of those approaches are equal. When we start to factor in reality and add in constraints, depending on the constraint, those approaches are not equal. If I asked for the cheapest way, then the response should be to walk. If I asked for the fastest way, then the response should be to fly. If I asked for the most efficient way, then the answer should be to take the bus or the train.

The solution or the idea we have to eventually solve a problem should be regarded in that same light. We should have an unwavering commitment to solving a desired problem and then be fluid in our approach to solving the problem. The real question we should be asking ourselves is: *How do we get to our final product or service?* The answer is simple: we need to monitor and evaluate how the end users, whomever they may be, respond to the latest iteration of our product. This is done through observations, surveys, focus groups, informational interviews, calls, etc. As entrepreneurs, we need to decide at what junctures we are going to stop to process the results and iterate to release the next version of our product or service. At Practice Makes Perfect, we do this once a year at the end of the summer. For Apple's iPhone, right after they release their latest model they begin working on releasing their next one.

Ultimately, evaluating and collecting information to improve our product or service is only worthwhile if we are ready to change our approach. When I originally came up with the mentoring model for Practice Makes Perfect, I decided to pair academically struggling students with higher-achieving near-peer mentors in a 2:1 ratio. It was not until the end of our second summer that we noticed how arbitrarily we picked the pairings. I remember talking to one of our advisors and suggesting a 1:1 ratio, and his response was, "One-on-one is awkward," so we decided to go with a two-on-one approach. The decision-making process in the latter half was not any better than it had been in the former case.

During the summer of 2013, we threw all of our arbitrary assumptions out the window and paired kids in groups that ranged from one-on-one to six-on-one to decide what the optimal group size was. We were only interested in having the maximum impact on the lives of the students we served. To our surprise, we found that four-on-one was the optimal group size, and that three-on-one and five-on-one were better than one-on-one.

Once we knew that those larger group sizes drove better outcomes, the next step was to figure out why—especially since it did not make sense intuitively at first. We discovered that when there were smaller group sizes there were more mentors in the classes and they would talk to one another once their scholars finished their work, which made classroom management tougher for our teachers. When the group sizes were a little larger, the mentors felt like teacher's assistants and the kids would compete amongst one another in their groups to get their work done.

Every summer since then, we have paid close attention to the feedback we received from all of the stakeholders who benefit from our program. We also realized we cannot just make changes in isolation. When we adjust our program schedule or change the curriculum, we monitor what the impact is on our programs.

The feedback over the years has influenced other parts of our programs as well. Over time, we have changed the number of college students in the classes, modified the role of the teacher, manipulated the duration of our programs, and revised our content. We have started and stopped a merit-pay program, and we have integrated home visits and modified them to meet the constraints that we are dealt. Sometimes we find that one approach works really well when our organization is a certain size; however, as we scale, that approach is no longer the best approach. As we continue to grow and scale our impact, we will continue to monitor the progress of our summer solution and iterate. That is because we are married to the impact and not the idea.

Chapter Ten

ENTREPRENEUR MINDSET

"Conquer your mind and conquer the world."
—Guru Nanak

In the process of building Practice Makes Perfect, I've realized there are three different mindsets I've adopted that have been vital to my success: going in the right direction, not now, and being wrong.

1. The "this is the right direction" mindset:

The right direction mindset is necessary when decisions have to be made with time constraints. It is an especially important mindset at times of uncertainty, which, for every entrepreneur I know, happens a lot. This mindset works well when the team or company is smaller and you're making decisions within your realm of expertise. You also need this mindset to take your vision from ideation to existence. That said, be careful getting too caught up in this mindset as your team grows. You will have other smart leaders (if you're hiring correctly), and the right direction needs to come from the group. In my experience, it isn't the right answer that typically works out. The answer or direction the group believes in, whether it is flawed or not, tends be the right answer.

2. The "*no* doesn't mean 'no'; it just means 'not now'" mindset:

First of all, you can't take "no" personally. Getting rejected is part of the entrepreneurial journey and learning process. I remember counting noes at one point early on in my journey and noticed that I was receiving ninety-seven noes for every three yeses. We kept moving and didn't let the negativity distract us. Eventually we would get yeses.

In the beginning, many of the noes really were "not nows." In future years, we converted several people who had previously said no to say yes.

Be careful not to get too carried away. No definitely does NOT mean yes or maybe. If you push too hard, you can alienate people and sever relationships. Instead, I'd suggest that when people say no you give them some space and later ask them for feedback on why they said it, if it wasn't inherently obvious. Use questions like: "Why did you decide against purchasing our product or using our service?" and "What would make you, or would've made you, a yes?

3. The "I was wrong" mindset:

No one wants to work for someone who thinks they are perfect and never admits when they are wrong. It shows a strong sense of insecurity and lack of awareness. The worst thing about being wrong and not owning up to it is that it sets the wrong precedent internally. If you, as the leader, don't admit when you're wrong, then others, internally, may never do it either. This means people will not be growing from their mistakes. At times, small issues may snowball into even bigger concerns.

There are also positive outcomes to admitting when you're wrong. For one, it shows a bit of vulnerability. It humanizes you. Also, owning your mistakes can be very powerful for company culture and getting help.

But be careful not to get too carried away with admitting when you're wrong. Not many people want to work for someone who is always wrong.

Chapter Eleven

DEALING WITH ROADBLOCKS

"Obstacles are put in your way to see if what you want is really worth fighting for."
—Author unknown

Every stage of running a company has its own highs and lows. In the very beginning, you're bootstrapping as you test your assumptions and build a minimum viable product. After getting a product out there and gauging feedback, you need to learn how and when to pivot. Once you pass the pilot phase and you start hiring people, you learn about the challenges associated with attracting, retaining, and rewarding talented individuals. In all of these areas, there are well-documented practices on how to avoid immediate failure. But what happens when your business is moving smoothly, the vision for the future is crystal clear, and you hit a wall?

A wall in this case isn't a funding gap or crisis; rather, think of it as a moment in time where you have a few options for next steps that all seem relatively attractive, but you can't support any of them with any logical reason. The reasoning needs to not only be rational but it has to make sense for your company too.

We recently had one of those moments at Practice Makes Perfect. Our goal of building a national summer school model was crystal clear, but the next step toward expansion in our growth phase was not. Did we need to replicate our model in every major city? Did we need to fully concentrate in a single state or city? There have been successful organizations that have done both. And after weeks of conversations held internally and externally, we broke through the wall and put together a game plan that made our next steps as clear as our end goal.

Here's how you can break through the wall and feel confident:

1. Define the roadblock.

What is your exact challenge? What are the obvious options? The most important things we did were reflecting and clearly articulating what we were up against. We then spent time talking and mapping the potential routes we could take. This makes it a lot easier to find a solution and gather feedback.

2. Identify the experts in your market or space.

This is where your board, investors, and extended network are most important. The easiest way for them to add value is by opening doors. Who are the thought leaders in your space? Once you've identified them, put in some extra effort identifying how you want to articulate the roadblock. The true experts in your field will have very little time, and you will have to get straight to the point. The only caveat here is that you don't want the list of people you need to speak with to be too long. For us, three to five was a good number.

3. Don't rush the decision.

Hopefully, you do not face too many roadblocks or walls in the really early days of starting your business. In this case, time needs to be your best friend, since this decision impacts your organization's strategic approach to scale and growth. Don't impose a deadline for when you need to come to a conclusion. When you have given it enough thought and spoken to enough experts, the right path for your business will become apparent.

The one reoccurring piece of advice we have received from our most knowledgeable mentors has been that you know your business better than anyone else. This is another defining moment where you have to make a decision with adequate information to ensure your company continues to thrive.

Chapter Twelve

Avoiding Burnouts

"Taking care of yourself doesn't mean me first,
it means me too."
—L. R. Knost

I believe the number one reason so many of the people in my purpose-driven realm have burned out is because they did not align their life expectations with what their purpose-driven work could provide. I know this because I have grappled with this along my journey.

A mentor of mine once told me that, in order to sustain the passion that I needed to have for my work, I needed to make sure I was sustaining myself. This is often a sore subject when it comes to dealing with social entrepreneurs and nonprofit founders because it deals with money, which is the last of the motivations on our list for why we committed to doing this work. At some point, we have to face the pressures of reality and understand that the things we want for ourselves and others have a price.

My mentor asked me simple questions about the number of kids I would like to have one day, how I would like to raise my family (middle class, upper-middle class, rich, etc.), whether I would send my kids to public school or private school, how much I would have to support my mom with her retirement, and how much income I wanted when I retired. To my surprise, I had answers for most of those questions. They might not have been final or exact, but I had an idea. He then asked me to do the math.

In 2009, *Time* magazine estimated the cost of raising a kid from birth to college was just north of $1 million. If you want to have three or four kids, that is a price tag of almost $5 million on its own. Buying a house in an upper-middle-class neighborhood could cost almost $1 million. If you factor in retirement and trying to sustain a six-figure income, that would mean putting away almost $2 million in retirement per person. The numbers quickly add up.

For weeks, I was saddled with frustration. I knew that as the executive director of Practice Makes Perfect I would never earn what I needed to achieve the goals and desires I wanted for myself and my family. Before I knew it, the work I loved so much, that had meant so much to me, started to mean less. There were moments when I resented my work because it meant I would never fulfill my wants. Like many of my friends, I toyed with the idea of leaving my work in search of work that might be less fulfilling, less purpose-driven, but might allow me to earn what I needed to bring to fruition the things I've wanted for myself and for my family my entire life.

After months of frustration, I finally understood why so many of my older peers in the space had not lasted very long. It was not that they did not love their work or that they were no longer able to carry it out; it was that they probably came to the realization I came to about their wants and their needs much sooner than I did, and because they were older than I was, they had less time to respond and react to their realizations.

When you reach the juncture I hit, you have one of four decisions to make. The first decision you could make is to keep things the way they are. You realize that you will never achieve the things you want for yourself and your family. If you do this, you will resent your work for depriving of you those wants you've had your entire life and you will burnout. The second decision you could make is to suppress your wants. You can reevaluate the things you have wanted your entire life and calibrate them to fall in line with what you are capable of achieving on the income you can reasonably expect to earn, which will help you avoid burning out and continue to keep you satisfied with your life. The third decision you can make is to restructure what you are doing in a way that will allow you to achieve what you've wanted and potentially leave the work you were so passionate behind you and potentially also cause you to burnout. The last decision, albeit the riskiest to consider, is to evolve what you're doing to meet your needs and your wants, which will help you avoid burning out as well.

I had an incredible amount of conviction in why I was doing the work I was carrying out. It ultimately led me to take Practice Makes Perfect private. I made the fourth decision. For people with less of an appetite for risk, I advise them to consider the second decision. I did not succumb to the belief that doing good means that you can't do well for yourself and that doing well for yourself means that you can't do good for the world. I did not accept the idea that you have to do well now so you can do good later in your life. I put my faith into my own hands and have continued to scale Practice Makes Perfect with a million plus in revenue each year for the last three years. In the process, I risked losing everything I had built. For some strange reason, I had faith it would all work out.

The first half of this chapter covered the mental part of the burnout journey. This second part is about the tactical part of avoiding burnout.

I am very far from having what some might consider an ideal work/life balance. Every once in a while, a friend or acquaintance asks how I avoid burning out. From my experience building Practice Makes Perfect from scratch, I know it takes a lot of time, energy, and sacrifice. The day you sign up to be an entrepreneur you are asking to be pushed toward burnout. Here's what I've learned that helps avoid burnouts:

- First, **create a routine**.

Start by putting together a frame of what you would like to achieve on an average day. There are plenty of templates you can find to spur ideas, but there is something special about owning this part of the planning. This part starts with your goals. If you do not set your goals, it will be hard to create a routine that you truly feel ownership over. Design your routine with ideal start and end times that help meet your daily needs

- Second, **add variety**.

As you are designing your days, make sure that they consist of different tasks. I cannot imagine doing the same exact things every single day. If you go to the gym, make sure you change the workout up. If you are at the office, change where you do work. Whatever it is you decide to do, avoid monotonous days by adding variety to your routine. Otherwise, you will get bored and may burn out very quickly.

- Lastly, **follow your routine religiously**.

This is probably the hardest part, especially when you don't have full control over your environment, such as when you are traveling. You may not have access to a gym, or there may be flight delays that cause you to make compromises to your regimen. However, when you are not traveling, this should be simple. When you finally get in a groove, you also become a lot more efficient.

Of course, this is one of those "easier said than done" secrets. If you can own the process, you should be able to avoid burning out. This secret has worked for me for many years.

Chapter Thirteen

DISCOVER WHAT
HELPS YOU PERSIST

*"If you would not be forgotten as soon as you are dead, either write
something worth reading or do something worth writing."*
—Benjamin Franklin

One of my friends told me, "I've never thought seriously about
becoming an entrepreneur, so I'm very inspired that you took
that step so early on and did it for the sake of others, rather than
yourself."

It must have been during a point in my work season where the
pressure was starting to mount and things were not going as great
and dandy as I would have liked them to be. I quickly told her that I
sometimes wondered why anyone would want to be an entrepreneur.
There are a lot of glamourless things that go into it. I cannot imagine
someone going into entrepreneurship and succeeding at building
something meaningful if they were in it for their own selfish desire.
Yes, the reason has to move and compel you to act, but it has to be
about much more than just yourself. When I shared that response,
she responded, "What helps you to persist despite those things?"

That question I did not answer as quickly. I knew there was an element of purpose, but was there more? *Am I missing something in this conversation that goes beyond my own reflection?* After all, this conversation was about something much larger than education; it was about being an entrepreneur and starting and building a business. You need more than just passion and purpose to deal with the clunk and gunk of running a company. The business side of things can get ugly. It is where you have to think through compensation, benefits, evaluating people, tracking goals and outcomes, picking insurance providers, and employee grievances.

After days of reflection, I finally settled on what I believe drives me to go beyond just engaging in purpose-driven work and trying to build a purpose-driven company. There are three pieces: purpose, potential, and legacy.

This entire book has been about how to live a more purpose-driven life and how to engage in more purpose-driven work. To be engaged in your purpose means you have to believe beyond any reasonable doubt that the work you are doing is the reason you were put on this Earth. That is essential to taking on anything that others see as daunting and especially challenging. For me, I know beyond a reasonable doubt that I was put on this Earth to help alleviate the inequality in education. That is what drives my work and my reason for being involved in education.

The next piece for me was all about potential. My entire life has been defined by potential. When I got to college, I heard the famous quote "talent is everywhere, even though opportunity is not." I was surrounded by bodies of research that made it clear that I had defied significant odds to be where I was at that moment. I started to become fascinated by human potential. If—given the right support at the right time—I was capable of producing Practice Makes Perfect and having the impact that I had on my community, what would it look like if I could help other people unleash their potential within my company? Building and growing a business provides me with the opportunity to do that within my company.

The third piece for me is all about legacy. I chose to commit myself to doing work that was about something much greater than myself. It was about other people. It was about creating opportunity. And it was about giving everyone an equal chance. It was about influencing policy and informing legislation.

Because building a purpose-driven company is so much harder than just being engaged in purpose-driven work, it helps to have these other motivations that are pushing you, especially in those moments where you find yourself doubting your purpose or when you have been given a reason to believe that the work you are doing is only out of passion.

Part III: *Starting*

Not every passion or purpose project should manifest itself into an organization or a company. In fact, I have many friends who are driven by their life's purpose and work on projects in a lab, in government, and in large corporations. Here are a couple of things to consider before you decide if this is a project worth building a new organization or company:

- **Scope**

   Start by giving thought to how large the impact is that you would like to have. Begin to think about the number of people you want to impact. Give some thought to how long you want to impact them for and how much that will cost. Ask yourself if you could imagine having several people working on your efforts full time.

If you decide you want to start a volunteer mentoring program between college students and local high school students for one summer, you probably don't need to start a nonprofit. If you decide you want to provide three-year job training for dozens of formerly incarcerated people, then you should probably incorporate and apply for tax-exempt status.

• Funding

Most of the time, when people ask me if they should incorporate a nonprofit, it is because they want to raise money to support their cause later that week or that summer. They come to me with a sense of urgency. They believe that foundations and individuals won't fund them until they have a 501(c)(3) status, and once they receive that designation and put in a little bit of work, that funding will start to come in from individuals, foundations, and corporations. It took us over a year to get incorporated and receive our exempt status. That didn't stop us from soliciting people for support. When you're starting out, the donations you're likely to get will be under $500, which for most people doesn't have a large impact on their taxes.

People will support you because they believe in you and the work you're trying to carry out, not because of a tax deduction. You won't get funding from a foundation or a corporation, but most of them won't give you money immediately after you have your 501(c)(3) either. They care more about your governance and alignment. Those are things you can work on without tax-exempt status.

If urgency of funding is what is driving your desire to get tax-exempt status, consider crowdfunding through a site like Indiegogo, Crowdrise, or GoFundMe. You don't need to be a tax-exempt organization and you can customize your profile to share your story. I highly encourage crowdfunding or peer-to-peer fundraising if it is going to be a short-term project or eventually become a nonprofit. If you're on the fence and have an opportunity to collect funding from a foundation or a corporation, consider finding a fiscal sponsor. Organizations like Social Good, Net Roots Foundation, or TSNE allow you to use their tax-exempt status to receive donations and provide your donors or funders with a tax deduction. I encourage most organizations, projects, or nonprofits to seek out fiscal sponsorship during the early stages of their development.

Chapter Fourteen

THE VERY BEGINNING

"The way to get started is to quit talking and begin doing."
—Walt Disney

How do you start? This is undoubtedly the first question I always get from people who are interested in starting their own businesses but haven't taken the leap yet. Most of the time, they have an idea they have been toying with for a few weeks or a few years. Some of them may have gone as far as registering a domain or even incorporating an LLC.

The very first step I tell people to take is to write their idea down on paper. Most of the time, your idea is just in your head. When it is in your head, you cannot really share it with anyone. Also, there are some ideas that sound really good in our heads but do not make a lot of sense when we put them on paper. Writing the idea down forces you to communicate what you were thinking on paper. It also sets you up for the next step.

Share your written idea with people. Make a list of four to five close friends or entrepreneurs and ask them if they'd be willing to review your idea and give you some feedback. Their initial review will likely turn up some interesting results. Sometimes you might find out that your ideas are actually not that unique; in fact, someone else has already created what you want to create. The bad news is that you no longer have a business. The good news is that you might just have to find another angle.

The most common reason people give me for why they have not shared their ideas with anyone else is because they were afraid someone else would take their idea and run with it. I don't know what movie or television show gave people this idea, but this is very seldom the reality. Building a business is hard work.

Most entrepreneurs will tell you, ideas are second to execution in business. You can have a great idea, but with poor execution, you will not get anywhere. Similarly, a bad idea with great execution has a better chance of succeeding.

When I was starting Practice Makes Perfect, I shared my idea with more than 200 different people via email, in-person conversations, and business pitches. Today, my idea has been shared with millions of people. Nothing has been stolen or profited off of in a way that has hindered my own ability to succeed or scale my own business. In fact, my original idea for Practice Makes Perfect would have probably failed. Part of building a business is being able to adapt. That's exactly what we did. My idea got better because of the input I have received from others since we started.

Once you have shared your idea with enough people and you have a strong sense that it is a great idea waiting to be unleashed, the next step is to figure out how to test your idea with as little money as possible. At this point, all you need to do is make sure that your assumptions are true. My team ran the first Practice Makes Perfect program on $10,000, which now costs $30,000 to run. We used volunteers instead of paid labor, and we paid stipends instead of an hourly rate. We leveraged friends' time to build a website, and we didn't worry too much about having fancy fliers or business cards.

We ultimately wanted to see if what we were doing was valuable.

If your idea creates value on a shoestring budget, then you know there's hope that it could create more value at a larger scale. If your idea does not create value in its minimal form, odds are it is not going to add a tremendous amount of value at a larger scale; of course, there are always exceptions.

The last step of the starting phase is to edit your initial idea on paper to reflect what you learned from feedback and from your test. Then you can summarize it in a one-page document that includes the idea and how much money you need to take the next step. This should be a document you can share with potential partners and investors.

Chapter Fifteen

ORDER OF
OPERATIONS

"Don't put the cart before the horse."
—John Heywood

Just recently, a friend asked me how I started Practice Makes Perfect. After being unable to readily answer him, I thought it must be a result of one of two things: there were too many possible ways to answer this question, or that starting companies has become so natural that I don't have to think about it anymore—it's like breathing or blinking. A quick moment of reflection proved the former to be true.

I realized that a lot of people try to start companies backward—that is, with the final step first. The actual incorporation, the documents to register with your state, should be that last thing you worry about. I have had friends who put really good ideas to the side because they didn't know how to incorporate a company or were worried about how they would find money to pay lawyers to help them get through the legal recognition phase.

The main reason entrepreneurial ventures fail is because of a lack of execution. I started my first venture at the age of thirteen.

In hindsight, my internet startup failed because I was missing the most important ingredient in running a company: other people. This included customers, cofounders, and investors.

The value of supporters cannot be underestimated. In fact, the most important of all people is your first supporter. Oftentimes, too much credit is given to the original idea generator. Yes, it's true that they had to persuade the first person to buy in, but it is the first follower who signals to everyone else that you may be working on something interesting.

Once you have an idea and a support team, you're well on your way. A business is informally born when a group of people provide a product or service consistently. At this point, the most important thing to do is to figure out your competitive advantage. This phase is all about identifying what it is about your product or service that will ensure its existence.

The final thing you need to do to make things official is to incorporate. I highly suggest putting this part off until you are certain that you want to pursue the business you are working on. Filing with the state and gathering articles of incorporation can be time consuming, and if you decide to pay a lawyer, the early expenses could slow your growth. Ultimately, expenses should be kept minimal with any startup venture.

Chapter Sixteen

Starting Up Lean

"Don't be in a rush to get big. Be in a rush to have a great product."
—Eric Ries

With so many changes still to be faced and iterations of your idea yet to come, you don't want to spend a disproportionate amount of your time creating bureaucracy and processes that you will only end up changing. Looking back, there are a handful of things that we did at Practice Makes Perfect when we first started out that we would never do as an established company. However, I can't imagine getting our business to where it is today without having done them. The beginning is all about the lean startup, and there are some things you can delay when starting lean.

1. Payroll provider:

Trying to be too legitimate from day one means you're going to burn more cash. We didn't start with a payroll provider until we had our second hire a few months into his role. Though doing payroll gets easier when you have a company calculating the deferrals and the taxes to withhold, it also comes with a hefty monthly fee and additional transaction costs. I have friends who have started companies and gotten up to five people before they actually signed on to a payroll provider. I don't know that I would've waited that long, but I know for sure it is one of those things you can put off for a bit.

2. Your dream domain name:

It would be nice to have your dream domain name from the start of your business, but the truth is that something close to it is perfectly fine to begin with. Since we had a common phrase as our company name, we quickly put ourselves in a boat where our domain wouldn't be available at a normal rate. Instead of buying the "practice makes perfect" domain at the very beginning, we settled for www.pmpnyc.org. We didn't actually buy the domain we wanted until we were two and half years into the company's development. Luckily, we were able to get it for $800 when we were ready. It wasn't terrible, but was still more than you should spend on a domain name when you first start a business.

3. Team member professional development:

As a smaller company, you can generally get away without a formal professional development policy. However, as you start to get bigger, you need to put a plan in place for how people will access resources within the company to grow and develop.

At the beginning it is also rare to get a person who fits the company culture and has all of the skills to do their job with the amount of compensation you're able to offer. Training helps fill the skill gaps.

4. Company phones and computers:

If not getting a company computer or phone isn't obvious to the new team member, they probably don't know they are interviewing at a startup. For every single hire we made up to our seventh or eighth one, we reminded them to bring their own laptop to work on day one. This saved the company the overhead cost of purchasing and having to account for any hardware. As you get larger, your teammates expect the company to provide the tools that they need to be able to do their job effectively.

Some of the corners we cut in the beginning would make me cringe if we cut them today, but they were essential for a faster launch. Today we dot almost every *i* and cross almost every *t*, but it is absolutely okay not to start that way.

※

Chapter Seventeen

Building a Strong Founding Team

"If you want to go fast, go alone. If you want to go far, go together."
—African proverb

Think you can do it alone? Think again. The last thing you want to do is try to launch a venture on your own. Having a team can speed up your startup's timeline, and it sends a signal to potential investors that you can persuade other people to believe in your idea. This skill is significant. Imagine an entrepreneur who can't persuade people to join his team trying to persuade a customer to buy his product.

Here are some pointers to help you build a stronger team:

1. Ask an advisor to join your team.
Starting a company with people is a lot like playing a team sport: there are competitions and funding pitches—some you'll win and others you'll lose. I believe it is essential to have a coach to have a successful team. By that logic, it doesn't make sense to try to build a business team without an advisor. Find someone

in your network, a friend, a mentor, or even someone you might just know who has had experience building a successful business (success marks in business to look for: being operational for more than ten years, selling a company for $5 million or more, doing several million in revenue annually, etc.). Make a list of eight to ten to start with; then narrow that list down in half to only those that you think might truly care about what you're building because they have some personal connection to you or what you are trying to do. Then reach out to them to see if they would be willing to meet with you or check in via phone every two to three weeks and be on call as you work on building your business.

2. Ask for input on decisions that haven't already been made.

When you are heading up a company, there will be several instances where you will have to react on the spot or make an obvious decision. It doesn't make sense to bring the entire team together to ask for their input. An update through email is usually sufficient for small decisions. However, make sure you always consult your team for larger decisions.

3. Never ask anyone on your team to do something you wouldn't do.

This tip is more than just literal. You shouldn't give others on your team work just because you do not want to do it or would not enjoy doing it. Odds are they won't enjoy it either. Instead, give them work because you need their help or you can't do it.

4. Entrust key tasks to those who have the skills.

In a small startup, early team members must be well versed at several things or at least willing to learn how to function in different roles. If you ask someone to do something that they don't know how to do, they may lose motivation. Or, if they're unwilling to learn, that's a red flag.

5. Delegate key tasks as evenly as possible.

It's hard to provide people an even amount of work, because they often have very different work styles and timelines. However, you can distribute work in a value-oriented way. For example, having a teammate focus specifically on your website is just as valuable to a startup as having someone focused on managing its finances. Both are valuable, but the upfront and maintenance work is very different.

6. Notice the small things that show you care.

I'm really big on birthdays. Really early on with our founding team, I would always recognize when it was one of our teammate's birthdays. It doesn't necessarily have to be birthdays, but find something personal that shows you care.

As you can see, the small details are what can easily make a difference. If you want to build a strong team that stays by your side, then focus on the small details as well as the large.

Chapter Eighteen

RAISING FUNDS

"Imbue your money with soul, your soul, and let it stand for who you are,
your love, your heart, your work and your humanity."
—Lynn Twist

I gave a presentation at the Global Good Fund Conference in DC on how I raised $2 million in two years, and that event generated dozens of questions on how I did it and what I learned.

There are thousands of organizations in the world that are doing incredibly impactful work, and people are being solicited by them all the time. Your job isn't just to demonstrate to people that your mission is important but to also prove to them that their donation is going to have more of an impact on the work you're doing than it will at one of the other organizations they could potentially be giving to.

Here are some of the most important aspects I've learned about raising funds:

1. The majority of giving in the United States comes from individuals.

This takes a little while to sink in. Most new nonprofit founders come up to me and ask me about the secret to getting grants and how we got all of the grants we needed to fund our organization. There are usually a few things that are wrong with that. First, they are assuming that the majority of our funding came from grants, which, in fact, is not the case. More than 50 percent of our funds raised came from individuals. I came across this mini-blurb in my fundraising journey, and it drastically changed how my team allocated its time within fundraising:

> *According to Giving USA's Annual Report on Philanthropy, in the year 2000, more than $200 billion was given to the not-for-profit sector. Of that $200 billion, only 5% came from corporations, 7% from foundations, and 80% from individuals. The bulk of the giving comes from individuals, and from those people who give 88% of the money, 75% of them made less than $150,000 yearly.*

Second, most foundations don't make hundreds of grants a year. They tend to have a portfolio of organizations they give to or support, and they continue to support them year after year. Unless the amount of money in the foundation increases, they usually don't look for new organizations. With that said, if there is an individual who emphatically believes in your work and they happen to sit on a foundation board, you can bypass most of the traditional bureaucracy involved with getting money.

2. You don't need to have a nonprofit status or a 501(c)(3) to start raising money from individuals.

I strongly advise that organizations consider finding a fiscal sponsor. Having a fiscal sponsor allows organizations to leverage another nonprofit's tax-exempt status to take on donations from individuals.

3. When you've met one individual, you've met one individual.

Everyone gives for different reasons, and the level of involvement and engagement they want to have is also different. One of the biggest mistakes you can make is trying to treat two people in the same way or using the same method to get two different people to donate.

4. Communication trumps impact.

This is a sad truth. You don't have to like it, but you have to appreciate it if you're going to be successful at fundraising. If you do incredible work and no one hears about it, then it is rarely going to get the funding that it needs. I've heard horror stories of organizations that have had very little impact, yet had incredible storytellers and communicators who brought in way more money to support their work.

5. People give to people not necessarily causes, especially in the very beginning.

Trust is the most important quality to exude. Having strong leadership within an organization is important. The leaders of an organization have to be able to deliver results and impact. In the earlier days of an organization, before the viability of the concept is proven, people are investing in the founder and the leadership team. You have to be willing and able to ask people for money to support your mission. More importantly, you need to connect with the people who are giving you money. Even though the person making a donation is giving to support a cause, they know that it is a person who is leading the charge.

6. Friends asking friends is powerful.

Building off of the last lesson learned, when people ask their friends to support a cause they are donating to, they are more likely to give than if they get a solicitation from an organization. It is also much harder to say no to your friend, who is a real person, than it is to say no to an inanimate thing (the organization in this case). There is a huge body of research as well as consulting companies out there that help advise organizations on fundraising from friends. They call the field "peer-to-peer" fundraising.

7. Fundraising is like sales.

You have to convince people that your work is worth supporting. More importantly, you have to follow up. Persistence is key. Most people don't like to think about giving away money, so they have to be constantly reminded that it is the right thing to do and that your organization is the right place to give the money.

Recently, the team at Signals by Hubspot launched an entire SlideShare based on the Referral Squirrel data, and the results showed:

2% of sales are made on the first contact.
3% of sales are made on the second contact.
5% of sales are made on the third contact.
10% of sales are made on the fourth contact.
80% of sales are made on the fifth to twelfth contact.

However:

48% of salespeople never follow up with a prospect.
25% of salespeople make a second contact and stop.
12% of salespeople make three contacts and stop.
Only 10% of sales people make more than three contacts with a prospect.

8. The Benevon Model works.

If you don't know what the Benevon Model is, quickly look it up. In essence, it is great for helping you build your network through "friendraisers" if you don't have a particularly large network. If you have a large network already, this model can have an exponential effect on your giving. It also allows other people within your circle of friends to get involved with your work.

9. Diversifying your funding streams does not increase your odds of succeeding.

In 2007, Stanford published a study that showed that more than 200,000 nonprofits had been started in the US since 1970, but only 144 of them had reached $50 million in annual revenue. Contrary to common logic around diversification, they actually raised the bulk of their money from a single type of funder, and they built professional organizations that were tailored to the needs of their primary funding source. I highly encourage people who are starting to think about growing their nonprofits to read these three *Stanford Social Innovation Review* articles: "Ten Nonprofit Funding Models," "Finding Your Funding Model," and "How Nonprofits Get Really Big."

10. Hiring a development person too early is a waste of money.

When you're first starting an organization, people don't want to meet with your development person. (For those not in the nonprofit space, development is another term for a fundraising professional.) They want to meet with the founder. They want to hear about your vision and why you're taking on this risk and sacrifice. What will ultimately wind up happening if you hire a development person too early is that they will just become an overpaid assistant. They will be reaching out to people in your network with very little success. Trust me, I made this mistake. Instead, hire an assistant to help you free up your time from menial tasks so you can focus your energy on building relationships and engaging more people in your mission.

11. When you can't get in touch with someone, handwrite them a letter.

With the hundreds of emails super-busy people receive every single day, doing something unconventional like handwriting a letter will almost always get you an answer. I don't advise you hand write a letter to a hundred people or anything like that.

Instead, target three to five people who you think would be compelled by your work or mission based on what you know about them, and make sure you have some sort of connection to them (i.e., same alma mater, similar interests, crossed paths somewhere before, etc.). Then write them requesting a meeting. If they take the time from their super-busy schedules to talk, they are already signaling that they are invested.

12. Learning is the key to success.

You need to be actively learning and seeking out resources. I'm only in a position to be able to provide this information with you all because I've taken the time to seek it out. The field is always changing, and new innovations will continue to disrupt how things are done. A few of the lessons here should stand the test of time, but many of these may not be relevant in five or ten years. Also, for every one resource I mentioned here, I've easily gone through fifty others. Make sure you continue learning!

PART IV: *PEOPLE*

All big things start small, and nothing impactful gets done alone. Practice Makes Perfect only got to where it is today because of other people. We are not a flashy tech startup. In fact, we're probably the furthest thing from that. At the peak of our seasonal employment, we employ almost 400 people in a single summer. We are a people-driven company. And I'm proud of that.

However, dealing with people does not come without its challenges. If you don't effectively manage your people, they will manage you. I've spent many a night stressing about inaccurate reviews on Glassdoor from disgruntled employees (only to realize that every business gets them), I've spent hours coaching employees who no longer wanted to work at our company, and I've spent tens of thousands of dollars on benefits to take care of my people.

You need the right people to run a business, but finding, utilizing, and managing them is never easy. This next section covers the very beginning of the people journey. It touches everything from hiring your first employee to onboarding them so they are set up to succeed, and working with interns to get them to add value.

Chapter Nineteen

THE HIRING PROCESS

"Hiring the best is your most important task."
—Steve Jobs

The one thing the best companies in the world understand is that their people are their most valuable assets. That rings especially true in a service-based business.

Some of the largest challenges at Practice Makes Perfect have been addressed by bringing the entire team together and brainstorming solutions. I don't think there is a single organizational problem that can't be solved if you have enough smart and committed people sitting at the table. Knowing that the biggest and most important decision you can make is hiring the right people means that all CEOs should be prioritizing their time to make the right hires.

Unfortunately, operating a business often gets in the way of desired priorities. So how do you own your company's most important decision without having to vet every single candidate?

1. Clearly articulate your company's values.

This is one of the most important things you can do, especially when you have a small team! The values and, more importantly, the behaviors that define your values will say a lot to a prospective employee about your company. I've had friends apply and choose not to apply to a company based on their values. So pay special attention to creating the things that are important to you in the workplace.

2. Play an integral role in designing the hiring process.

This is your opportunity to create the hurdles that will keep "bad fits" from joining your team. Though it is important to play a large role, make sure you're not the sole voice in the design. The process you create will dictate how the interviews are conducted, what your team members will be looking for in potential employees, and will save you from interviewing every single candidate. People should only be able to get into your company by getting through the process you designed. The only exception we make is for people who have interned with us before. At that point, we've had enough time to evaluate whether or not they'd be a good cultural fit for our organization.

3. Make the final decision on all hires. No exceptions.

No ifs, ands, or buts. There is research that shows that a bad hire can cost as much as fifteen times their base salary. Not to mention that one really good hire often produces more value than three mediocre hires. That means getting it wrong can be costly and getting it right can actually be lucrative for your business. For every hire, we have put together a hiring committee of four people. We appoint a head of the committee who assembles a hiring packet for every candidate that they think should be hired. I get a hiring packet for every potential hire, and within a few minutes I can get a sense of the candidate and their abilities.

Letting your teammates know that you will be involved in every single hire sends the message that it is really important to you. More importantly, it means that you're likely to get people who are better fits for your company.

Chapter Twenty

THE FIRST HIRES

"When you are ready to make your first hires, look for people who under-stand your passion, want to add to your ideas and can envision ways to make improvements."
—Richard Branson

When I was ready to hire my first coworker at Practice Makes Perfect, I was focused on finding someone who shared my values, was interested in what our company was doing, and could manifest themselves through our work. As a result, I wound up hiring a colleague from Cornell University. By turning to my network, I had a solid understanding of what he would and would not know.

While going that route may have worked for me, it may not for others. That said, what I have learned is shared values and possessing a similar work ethic are extremely important. Obviously, the latter is difficult to know until they start working.

For many startups, besides being concerned about hiring the right fit, bringing on your first employee can be a financial burden. In my case, I knew I had to raise the individual's salary or come up with a strategic plan on how I was going to cover payroll.

For those ready to bring on their first employee, keep these aspects in mind:

- **Be transparent.**

Be up-front about your financial situation, and sell the person on the vision and growth trajectory of the organization. Often, people looking to work in startups are driven by more than money. If the startup is working on a mission they are passionate about, they may be willing to be on the ground floor and build up in lieu of a big salary.

- **Invest in your first hire.**

As an entrepreneur, you need to take the time to teach and develop your first employee. The faster they can understand your business and industry, the sooner they can add value to the work you are doing.

- **Look for a generalist.**

When bringing on employee number one, don't hire a specialist unless you absolutely have to for your startup. In my experience, I've found that having someone who is good at a few things is better than having a colleague who is an expert in one area.

- **Share responsibilities.**

If you plan on hiring someone and unloading all of your work, he may head for the door. No one wants to work somewhere they are going to be overworked, underpaid, and undervalued.

One of the easiest ways to show someone that you value them is to allow them to take on big responsibilities, but you have to share the big responsibilities with them.

Once you have your first hire on board and things are operating smoothly, you may find that it is time to begin hiring the rest of your team. This process should not be rushed. As you transition from a solo entrepreneur to a team player, here are some things to keep in mind:

- **Take responsibility for the big failures.**

Starting a company is a team game, as everyone has potential to lose something. But at the end of the day, the company is your baby. When a big loss occurs and you are to blame, don't point your finger at someone else. Quickly own up to your failures and take action to correct them.

- **Don't hastily propose problems.**

Time is money, and with only a few hires, these employees don't have a lot of it to waste.

There is a very thin line between looking for supporting solutions and already having a solution in mind. So make sure you articulate where you are in the problem-solving or decision-making process. People love to feel included and want to help. However, they don't like being taken on a ride or asked for their opinion if it clearly doesn't matter and the decision has been made or the problem has been solved.

- **Don't own all of the big decisions.**

The reality is that everyone will have to live with the consequences of your decisions, so they should be invited to help make the really big decisions. Because your team is small, make sure they have input (when applicable) and applaud their insight when it helps move your company forward.

- **Be vulnerable.**

Entrepreneurs don't have all the answers, especially first-time founders. That's okay. Your team would rather have you solicit input in the areas that you are experienced in than make the wrong decisions because you were scared to ask for help.

- **Bring your team to big meetings.**

When meeting with potential clients, vendors or partners, don't hesitate to include a hire or two. As long as they will be beneficial to the meeting, having your team involved can increase the level of inclusion at the organization and transparency around your work, and can save you time in the long run if you feel comfortable sending them off to the meetings on their own.

- **Listen and deliver.**

This is plain and simple. Don't just sit there and pretend you are hearing what your team is saying; show that you're listening. Offer feedback, ask smart questions, and if a team member's input can improve your business, act on it.

Chapter Twenty-one

THE WRONG HIRE

"Hire slow, fire fast."
—Michael Hyatt

Building a great mission-driven company with incredibly passionate people is the big picture. There was a time when the workload distracted me from this vision, and I rushed the hiring process.

During our hiring process, we settled on a candidate that came across as capable but not passionate. (I am almost convinced that passion is not something you can teach someone.) After weeks of lackluster performance, we decided to let this person go. It wasn't easy. Not only was it an expensive lesson but the process of letting someone go is mentally and emotionally draining.

When you hire someone for a role in a small company, you can't forget that you're also hiring him or her to be a brand ambassador. Their interactions with people and supporters may sometimes be the only impression they get of your company. Ultimately, every hire in your early stages should be just as passionate and invested in the success of the company as you are, because it directly impacts your startup's survival.

Here are some ways to avoid hiring the wrong person:

1. Avoid hiring full-time employees outright.

This is especially important for the first set of new hires who are outside of your immediate circle of professionals and whom you have not previously worked with.

Today, it is typical for companies to start individuals on a trial period. Thirty- to ninety-day trials are fairly common before making a final decision on their employment. This period provides you with an opportunity to gauge their passion for the job and overall group fit. Some people may come across as well polished and can feign interest during an interview, but it is a lot harder over a multi-week trial period.

2. Be patient.

This is probably the thing most entrepreneurs, myself included, struggle with most. We are all dreamers with big visions, and those ambitions cause us to set lofty goals. In our hearts, we know the goals are achievable, but sometimes they require just a little more help than we anticipated.

When we made our third hire, we were feeling a little overwhelmed, and we let that influence our decision-making process. Instead of looking to find the right person for our company—someone who shared the same mission, values, and capabilities—we found ourselves looking for a person who we believed was strictly capable of doing the work.

3. Implement a 100-percent rule for your first ten hires.

Until our team grows to more than ten people, everyone in the organization must approve anyone who is interested in joining our team for a full-time position. This will not only ensure that everyone is involved in the decision-making process, it will also increase everyone's commitment to the new team member's success within our organization. Onboarding an employee when you are busy is never easy, and it only becomes more challenging if not everyone has bought into their success.

These points are not likely to completely eliminate having to fire someone again, but hopefully they will increase your odds of making the right decision on your next big hire.

Chapter Twenty-two

UTILIZING INTERNS

"The expert at anything was once a beginner."
—Helen Hayes

A federal appeals court gave employers flexibility, once again, to use unpaid interns legally when the work serves an educational purpose. This decision overturned a lower court decision that made hiring unpaid interns for for-profit companies and nonprofit organizations incredibly difficult. The language surrounding the last ruling on what was deemed an acceptable unpaid internship was crystal clear and left very little room for misinterpretation. As a result, Practice Makes Perfect decided we wouldn't take on any interns unless we could compensate them. This meant fewer educational opportunities for students and less support for our growing organization. But the new ruling means we will have greater capacity to take on interns in the future and provide educational opportunities that will also aid our organization's growth.

With that said, more interns don't necessarily mean greater productivity. In fact, I've heard dozens of intern horror stories. For entrepreneurs starting out, interns can be your greatest ally or your biggest nightmare. Nonetheless, when we founded PMP, I was eighteen years old and was capable of adding value within an organization. My perspective gained from successfully interning at a few companies, and now having had several interns at PMP, has taught me that if you structure the opportunity correctly, it can in fact be mutually beneficial.

Here are ways to maximize your interns' effectiveness:

1. Assign them an internship project.

This is a long-term task that you'd like them to complete before their internship ends. On the intern's end, it will provide them with a self-directed opportunity to conduct research, ask questions, and have something to present. This could be an individual project or a project that multiple interns can share and work on together. This also helps when you're overwhelmed and don't have time to assign a new task or project. That way, the intern always has something they can work on.

2. Give them someone to report to at the company.

Make it clear who their manager is when they start. Interns should be encouraged to speak with anyone on your team, but they should also have someone they can go to in the event that others aren't available.

3. Make them feel included.

Do you have company-wide meetings? If so, include them in the conversations. We have a weekly team meeting where we discuss pressing challenges, and our interns are asked to attend. If you want them to act on information, then they should have full knowledge of the things that are happening. We also value transparency at our company.

4. Prepare a list of tasks.

This takes some time on your end but will help you in the long run. Before our interns started, we made a list of things we needed them to get done. That way, they could add value for us as well.

The reality is that not every intern is going to be great, so calibrate your expectations. Nine out of ten times it is the employer's fault for not adequately screening or providing the appropriate training.

The best interns find ways to add value without getting in your way or asking you for more work usually two to three weeks into their internships. With that said, if you do not invest the time during those first two weeks really explaining what you do and how it works, your interns won't feel empowered to add or create value.

I'm glad the courts overturned their previous position on unpaid internships. For me, internships were crucial to my skill development, and we need more of them in the workplace to train our next generation of leaders. Any constraints placed on those opportunities hurt our economy in the long run.

PART V: *STRUCTURE*

For-profit, not-for-profit, LLC, benefit corporation, etc.—all of those are just legal structures. Which one do you pick? Ultimately, you need to pick the one that will best position you to achieve your goal or mission. When I first started Practice Makes Perfect, I wanted to support low-income kids and families who were growing up in neighborhoods just like the one I was growing up in. In order to do that, I needed to raise money from people who had money and could support our services. The best way to do that in the United States is to be incorporated as 501(c)(3) nonprofit organization.

Later, I realized we were solving a problem for schools and they would be willing to pay to customize our solution. In this section, I'll detail how we went from a 501(c)(3) to a benefit corporation and why we did it, and I'll share some things to keep in mind as you consider different legal structures.

Chapter Twenty-three

Nonprofit vs. For-Profit

"You're the bridge between the pain point of where your customer is now and where they want to be."
—Mark Hudson

To provide low-income kids and families with free enrichment programs over the summer, we figured that we'd have to find a way to get people who have money to donate to our cause so we could provide the programs for free, since our target beneficiaries didn't have money.

To raise money at a large scale, we recognized that we needed our legal structure to be a 501(c)(3) nonprofit organization. After operating for a couple of years, we realized that if we were to have any chance at scaling our work to reach a critical number of children and families every summer, then we would have to get schools to contribute to support our programs. That was the beginning of our earned income strategy.

Nonprofits can have earned income models and remain non-profits. In fact, many hospitals and universities have earned income strategies and strategically remain nonprofits because it makes the most sense for them.

Here were the three reasons we decided to convert:

1. Social Problem vs. Pain Point:

Traditionally, nonprofits solve social problems, like home-lessness, poverty, and achievement gaps; and for-profits solve pain points, like finding a new apartment and learning a new skill to be successful at work.

In our case, we began to realize that our school part-ners were not paying for our services because they wanted to narrow the social problem of the achievement gap. Rather, they were paying for our services because they needed sup-port running summer programs. The way the school year was designed set them up for failure in trying to operate any summer programs effectively. Thus, we were operating in the realm of the for-profit space.

We also realized that we were in a space where we were competing with other for-profit companies, like Scholastic, Pearson, and McGraw Hill. However, we were limited to using nonprofit tools. At that point, we realized if we wanted to compete with other for-profit companies, we would have to be on a level playing field where we could operate with the same resources.

2. Market Opportunity:

This is probably the biggest factor driving your conversion, and it was ours too. When we started out, there was no such thing as a summer school market. It is still debatable whether one exists today. However, after generating millions in revenue in this space, we'd like to believe that there is in fact a market. Moreover, the market has the potential to be worth over $10 billion nationally. When we realized this market existed, we decided that if we remained a nonprofit, we wouldn't be as compelled to provide and deliver a service that actually met the needs of the market, because we'd always have philanthropy to rely on. By becoming a for-profit, we recognized that we'd have to be more responsive to our customers and provide something that was addressing a need for our partners. This was a lot more in line with the ethos of our company, which we'd been operating as a business from the very beginning.

3. Ownership:

When I originally started building Practice Makes Perfect, ownership was the last thing on my mind. The reforms we were carrying out were led by my firsthand perspective. I was empathetic to the challenges and the adversities that our kids faced. I was them.

Nonetheless, I would find myself backing down as I went toe-to-toe with our board as we were building the organization. Every board member on a 501(c)(3) board has equal voting power. That means the founder or the executive director cannot make decisions unilaterally. That's because most nonprofits are funded by individuals who receive a tax deduction for their contributions. Because those tax deductions are money that would've gone to the government, the government assumes ownership over the assets of any nonprofit. The board members are appointed fiduciaries who are supposed to act in the benefit of the government. What's in the best interest of the government may not always be what's in the best interest of the mission.

There were times when I found myself wanting to take bigger risks and make larger leaps to serve more students only to be told I needed to be "more realistic" or "not take on that level of risk." That's when I realized that ownership was important for me because it would maintain the integrity of the work my team was carrying out.

When we finally decided to make the conversion, we decided to become a benefit corporation.

Chapter Twenty-four

A Benefit Corporation

"It takes twenty years to build a reputation and five minutes to ruin it."
—Warren Buffett

The advantages of being a for-profit trying to achieve our mission of creating high-quality academic summer programs outweighed the advantages of being a nonprofit. In the process of making the conversion, we learned that not all for-profits are created equal. After several discussions with our leadership team, our board, and our lawyers, we decided to become a benefit corporation.

Benefit corporations, like B Corps, are for-profit companies that meet rigorous standards of social and environmental performance, accountability, and transparency. In essence, benefit corporations aspire to use the power of markets to solve social and environmental problems. When we were inspired to incorporate as a benefit corporation, here were our five reasons:

1. Shared Beliefs:

B Lab, which is the nonprofit group that holds benefit corporations and B Corps accountable, shared our belief that businesses should exist to do more than just turn a profit. We both believed that businesses should be used as a force for social good. At Practice Makes Perfect, one of our four core values is conscious capitalism, which is all about the triple bottom line. We know business principles can be used appropriately as a very powerful tool to address social inequities.

2. Community:

Every entrepreneur knows that building a business is hard work. It's even harder work when you're doing it alone. Today, there are over 2,000 B Corps around the world. B Lab aggregates learnings, shares case studies, provides professional development, and creates opportunities for CEOs to convene and engage in meaningful conversations.

3. Public Accountability:

The standards that benefit corporations and B Corps need to adhere to are the gold standard for how businesses should operate. As a company that worked directly with our public education system, we wanted to hold ourselves to the highest available standard of public accountability. B Lab's incorporation and certification process keeps companies honest.

4. Ability to Put Money Second to What Matters:

This was one of our top reasons. We didn't get in the business of eliminating the summer learning loss and working with low-income children just because we wanted to make a profit; otherwise, we would've incorporated as a for-profit from day one. We put mission first as a benefit corporation. This truly allows us to think about what is in the best interest of our kids and our school partners.

5. Attracting the Right People:

Being a benefit corporation or a B Corp gives you the opportunity to make a very public declaration that you care about more than profit. This is a signal to your investors, your customers, and your employees (both current and future) that you are more than just your numbers.

Being a benefit corporation or a B Corp isn't a walk in the park. The assessments take time, and they require a sincere commitment to doing right by ALL of your people—employees, customers, and shareholders. It also isn't free, but it's well worth the value if you take advantage of the 2,000+ member community that spans forty-two countries and over 120 industries.

Chapter Twenty-five

BEFORE CONVERTING A NONPROFIT TO A FOR-PROFIT

"Courage isn't a matter of not being frightened, you know. It's being afraid and doing what you have to do anyway."
—Jon Pertwee

Deciding to convert Practice Makes Perfect from a nonprofit to a for-profit public benefit corporation was one of the most challenging undertakings of my business career. Not only is restructuring a business incredibly difficult, but there were a few things I wish I had known before I embarked on the transition that caught me off guard. Before converting your business, consider the following:

1. Timing:

No one can really tell you how long the entire process is going to take. We had the best lawyers in the world during our conversion, and at one point they told us the process would take six to eight weeks. From previous experiences, we knew that lawyers tend to overpromise on timing, but nothing could've adequately prepared us to go through an almost eighteen-month process.

2. Fundraising:

We spent a lot of time trying to raise capital. One of our initial investors encouraged us to make the conversion and promised to support us through the transition. When we eventually started the process and went to this person for the capital, we realized we had never agreed on the terms of the investment (he wanted a percentage of our company), so we lost our lead investor. We realized our last option was to raise the money through our customers, and we were fortunate that this route worked out for us. We made the conversion successfully and didn't have to give up any control or ownership of our business.

3. People:

Be ready to have conversations around equity. This could make or break your company. I was ignorant to the notion that my teammates who originally came to work for a nonprofit would have strong opinions on how much equity they should receive in the newly formed company. It was difficult to distribute equity in a rational way. There are no good rulebooks or guidelines for how to do this properly. Equity distribution is more of an art than a science. But if you don't get the equity distribution right, you risk breaking your new company before it starts.

4. Banking:

Our banking relationships are where we got blindsided the most. The lines of credit and the credit history we had built with the nonprofit were pretty much disregarded. Banks don't traditionally work with companies that have less than two years of operating history. That's because the odds of failure are so much greater in the first couple of years. After months of discussions, negotiations, and raising alternative capital, we mended relations and got waivers to many of the rules. It also didn't hurt that we had done over $1 million in business within six months of our conversion.

5. Board:

For the conversion process to be perceived as in the best interest of the mission, your board members should not transition with the management team. In fact, there needs to be an "arms-length" transaction. This means that no one on the buyer's side should have influence on the board's final decision to sell or not sell the assets. If board members move to the for-profit side, it can be perceived as private inurement.

Unfortunately, board members on nonprofits are not compensated. As such, getting decisions made, having critical conversations, and having paperwork signed can sometimes drag the process. If you're a board member on the nonprofit side of the transaction, you have nothing to gain in the asset sale, but are taking on a risk by agreeing to the asset purchase, since this process is scrutinized closely by the Attorney General. And if the process goes smoothly, then you lose your board seat. If it weren't for the external support from one of the top legal firms in the world and the promise of financial support from a billionaire investor, I'm certain the board would've voted to table the discussion of a legal structure conversion. You need to be very thorough in making the case for the for-profit company to be able to better execute on the mission set forth by the nonprofit.

Making our conversion was a big commitment. We delivered on our initial promises, but sold an ambitious plan, and we're going to have to continue working toward fulfilling the rest of our promises. Today, I can confidently say that the decision to make the conversion was in the best interest of our mission, our people, and our kids.

Chapter Twenty-six

How to Convert a Nonprofit to a For-Profit

"Don't wait for the perfect moment, take the moment and make it perfect."
—Zoey Sayward

After my team made the decision to convert our legal status from a nonprofit to a for-profit, the next thing we needed to figure out was how. It is very easy to go from a for-profit to a nonprofit. Going the other way is not. After having gone through the process, I completely understand why.

In making the conversion happen, timing matters. Most of the founders I spoke to who had completed the conversion but failed after the fact stated that it was because they didn't find a product-market fit. They anticipated that their service or product could work for a for-profit business, and they jumped to make the conversion before they gained full acceptance of their product or service. However, if they had waited until the business was too mature, then the cost of converting the business might have outweighed the benefits.

Assuming you have the timing right, which is subjective and will vary across businesses, there are few options for how to convert a nonprofit to a for-profit. Below are the three most popular options, with pros and cons:

1. Licensing, Leasing, or Renting the Assets:

This requires you to set up a new legal entity that you can incorporate in any structure you want. Then you work with the board of the nonprofit to draft an agreement that will allow you to rent, license, or lease the assets that you need for the new company.

> **a. Pros:** This is quick and easy. It provides you with immediate access to the assets that you need to do business.

> **b. Cons:** You manage multiple entities. You do not own the assets outright. The board of the nonprofit can change its mind and terminate its agreement with you, which could put you out of business.

2. Complete Asset Purchase:

This option is the direction my team decided to go. This option requires you to set up a new legal entity that you can incorporate in any structure you want. Then you have to hire counsel to represent the management team (buyer) and counsel to represent the board (seller). Once the counsel is in place, then you have to hire an accounting firm to provide what they believe to be a fair market value of the assets. The value is determined based on conversations with the board, an evaluation of the balance sheet, and any hard assets that are being transferred. The management team then has to raise the money to purchase the assets. The board must approve the asset sale. Finally, the last approval must come from the Attorney General in the state where the transaction is taking place.

a. Pros: You own the assets once the process is approved.

b. Cons: This is the costliest of the different routes. This route also takes the longest of the three to accomplish.

3. Full Restart:

During the process of the asset purchase, I wished several times that I had gone down this route. This route requires you to start a new entity and start over. It means walking away from what you built. Nonetheless, the most valuable piece of the experience is what you learned. Sometimes that chance to start over means you could probably do it even better. This option is only available for companies that are providing a service. Most states have loose noncompete laws, which means anyone can start a competing business that copies exactly what you're doing without any penalty unless you have a patent. It would require you to change the name and the branding, but those things shouldn't be that valuable at the time of your conversion; otherwise, you've probably waited too long to make the switch.

a. Pros: This is the cheapest route to undertake. You do not need to hire any counsel and can pretty much walk away from what you have built to date.

b. Cons: The perception that you used donor assets to build something, get traction, and then use it with a profit motive is poor. However, if you're genuinely doing it for the greater good of the mission, you shouldn't care too much about that.

When my team and I made the decision to make our conversion, we only really knew of the first two options. The intricacies of making this conversion happen are complicated. Though you may not need counsel to go through the entire process, depending on the route you choose to go, you should consult counsel at the start of the process to evaluate if there are any other options for you to consider that may be specific to your business.

Part vi: *Operations*

Abusiness is a business is a business. I say that to say that all organizations—nonprofit, for-profit, LLC, benefit corporations, etc.—are all businesses in some form or fashion. They may not have the same goals of maximizing profits or of maximizing impact, but they all are run by people and governed by a set of laws, require strategy to be positioned for success, and require execution to be successful. Having operated the same company in two different legal structures, I know that those are all just legal designations. In both instances, I've had to take steps backward in order to move forward stronger. I've learned that *forward* isn't always *straight forward*. In this next section, I cover what I've learned about managing the early operations of a business.

Chapter Twenty-seven

CREATING A BUSINESS MODEL

"Luck is not a business model."
—Anthony Bourdain

For young entrepreneurs, your first order of business must absolutely be making sure your bright idea will pay off.

As a freshman in college, one of my professors told me that profits, marketing, location, and people are all important, but the real secret to any successful business is a great business model.

He then illustrated his point by way of the franchising industry: The most successful models, like Pizza Hut and McDonalds, for instance, are so simple to understand that, with minimal training, individuals of all stripes can operate the business. I often find myself echoing this wisdom when I chat with other budding entrepreneurs.

At Practice Makes Perfect, we partner with low-income schools across New York City to get them to outsource their summer learning programs to our team. We realized that over the summer kids in low-income neighborhoods forget what they have learned, while their middle-class peers make gains. We also noticed that schools struggle to execute and implement high-quality summer learning programs. Today, schools pay us to operate summer learning programs for their children, which prevents them from forgetting what they have learned and returning to school ready to succeed the following year.

My friends at Barnana realized that many farmers lost up to 20 percent of their bananas because they were no longer ripe or yellow. In an effort to reduce food waste, they started upcycling the bananas by creating tasty and nutritious snacks out of them. From a business standpoint, they are able to purchase food that would otherwise have been thrown out, which allows them access to lower food costs for a very similar end product. The more snacks they sell, the less food is wasted. They are well on their way to upcycling other foods.

When devising your business plan, keep these points in mind to ensure your business model is on track for success:

1. Does this business model make sense?

You may come into communication with investors through business plan competitions and other funding opportunities. Think about your business idea from their perspective. Would you willingly pour time, energy, and personal resources into your venture?

2. What do you do?

This is plain and simple: if your customers don't understand what you do or how you do it, they won't buy what you're selling. As soon as you have a minimum viable product, let everyone you know test it and tell you what they think. It's that early feedback that will be invaluable when you're trying to attract new customers.

3. Can others explain your model?

The people working for you need to be able to articulate your vision. They need to understand the value that your goods or services provide and why consumers should be purchasing them from you. A clear business model makes it easier for employees to communicate your business's value proposition.

4. Can the company break even?

Sustainability is crucial. Your business model must communicate how your company brings in revenue (or plans to bring in revenue) and covers its expenses. If the business model fails to do this, then your company won't last. Be sure you have a long-term growth plan in place for making money.

Once you've figured out the answers to these questions and can effectively implement them into your business model, you are on your way to building a scalable business.

Chapter Twenty-eight

KNOW WHEN TO PIVOT

"Write your principles in pen and your business model in pencil."
—Josh Kopelman

As almost every entrepreneur knows, the initial idea is never the end result. To ensure your startup doesn't fail, you need to make pivots to your plan based on feedback, knowledge, and variables out of your control.

Figuring out when and why to pivot is difficult. Here are a few insights I learned about changing gears along my entrepreneurial journey:

• **The gut-based pivot**:

These pivots are based on the founder or founding team's instincts. They are common earlier in the development of the business model.

When we were first putting together our concept for Practice Makes Perfect, we wanted to pay the high school mentors and the college interns minimum wage. The cost to operate the model for thirty students would have been almost $50,000. Our inability to raise the funds necessary to execute that model forced us to pivot or live with the idea of not existing. As a result, we discovered how to create value in nonmonetary ways by including test prep and college readiness support for our mentors, which allowed us to pay them a more modest stipend.

- **Research- and need-based pivots**:
These shifts are based on information that already exists.

When we ran our first program in 2011, we were serving fourth-grade and ninth-grade students. If we wanted to serve the bigger needs, we realized we would have to find a way to expand our programming or become obsolete. Donors and parents were asking us what would happen to our students after the summer. Instead of continuing to say we didn't know, we pivoted our model and expanded our services to support students from grades kindergarten through twelfth grade.

- **Experience- and evidence-based pivots**:
These pivots come from piloting and evaluating results.

For our first few summers, we experimented with different numbers of Teaching Fellows (college students who lead instruction) in our classrooms. We got to a point where we had two fellows in our elementary school classes and one in our middle and high school classes. After several years of running with this model, we noticed that the elementary school Teaching Fellows would always complain about how the workload was divided. There also weren't any meaningful differences in outcomes between our elementary and our middle and high school classes. After a couple of years of close monitoring, we shifted the model to include one Teaching Fellow across all of our classes.

- **Feedback-based pivots**:
These pivots are based on what your stakeholders suggest.

Depending on your line of business, time, and scope of work, you may or may not have the capacity to conduct extensive market surveys to identify your customers and how much they are willing and able to pay for your product or service.

Following our final pilot, we transitioned our organization's business model from one that relied heavily on philanthropy to one that relies on fees for service. As such, in trying to lock in the appropriate price point, we had several calls with charter school principals and public school leaders. Each potential customer provided feedback, and we ultimately decided the direction.

Chapter Twenty-nine

An Ideal
Workplace

"We're all working together; that's the secret."
—Sam Walton

Your business should do everything and anything it can do to take care of and protect its people. That means a laser focus on your mission and bottom line to ensure that you can maintain your sustainability. If you run out of cash or if you burn through money too quickly, you'll bring your mission and your dream to a dead end.

As Practice Makes Perfect continued to grow and evolve, so did my views on productivity and work. We realized that if we created an environment that expended people daily, we'd have two or maybe three years, if we were lucky, before they burned out. Armed with that knowledge, we knew we needed to make changes quickly or else we would lose the people we needed to solve our problem. As we started to think about hours spent and productivity, we considered what the total environment looked like. We wanted to build an incredible company that everyone would be proud to work for.

Benefits are attractive and may keep employees on board longer. However, a company that is around for the long term is more attractive than a company that exists for a couple of years with massive amounts of benefits. The first five items below are pretty standard, easy-to-implement items to consider in designing your company's benefit package. Items six through ten are advanced benefits that a startup should probably not implement right away, but should aim to implement in the long run.

1. Work Hours:

This makes a HUGE difference. Our office hours are 9:00 a.m.–5:30 p.m. People feel less guilty about leaving when they're supposed to leave. They also feel like they're going above and beyond just by staying thirty additional minutes, instead of having to stick around until midnight just to show how hard-working they are.

2. Federal Holidays:

This is an easy way to boost morale. Besides, if they have friends who aren't working because of the holiday, it demotivates them. Additionally, the federal government tends to do the closest Friday or Monday to the actual date giving people a three-day holiday. At Practice Makes Perfect, we take it a step further; we give people the days between Christmas and New Year's off too.

3. Unlimited Vacation:

This one is a bit tricky because research shows that people tend to take fewer days off when they have an unlimited vacation policy than when they don't. To combat that, we have two compulsory days off that every employee must preplan with their manager at the beginning of the quarter (not including federal holidays). We've been doing this for over a year now and haven't had a single case of abuse.

4. Work from Home:

We give our managers full discretion over this. I'll admit, this is one of the perks that I've struggled to fully embrace, because I like to see the people I'm working with. But working from home might be ideal for some people, based on their situations.

5. Work Essentials:

These things seem pretty basic, but we provide a monthly stipend for professional development, transportation, gym, and phone.

6. Total Health-Care Package:

We cover the entire health insurance premium for our staff members and their families, including dental and vision. We also provide life and disability insurance.

As we continue to think about our new benefit corporation designation, we want to continue pushing the envelope of being a company that puts its people first. Here's what we're hoping to meaningfully incorporate over the next few years:

7. Comprehensive Family Leave Policy:

We want our expecting parents to feel supported and encouraged.

8. Tuition Reimbursement:

Though our compensation and benefits are pretty comprehensive, we want to continue to support our team members' personal growth and development.

9. Home Purchase Assistance Program:

We want our team members to have the opportunity to fulfill the American Dream, and understand that the down payment can sometimes be a huge barrier to home ownership. We plan on providing team members with up to 20 percent of their initial down payment for their first home in the form of a forgivable loan that is paid down with service for our company.

10. Employee Stock Ownership Program:

A little more than 50 percent of our full-time team members have stock in the company. We'd love to formalize a program and get to a point where 100 percent of the people who work with us have the opportunity to own a piece of the company they are committed to building.

Full disclaimer: these perks are expensive. Instead of phasing them all in at once, you can add them in gradually. I think the startup industry could benefit greatly if we started to think about our longer-term impacts instead of our short-term profits to please an investor. There isn't anything revolutionary in here that companies can't do to put their people first.

Chapter Thirty

ACCOUNTABILITY

"Accountability is the glue that ties commitment to result."
—Bob Proctor

One of the toughest balances to achieve within an organization is between building a culture that gives people space while maintaining an environment of accountability. The line between managing and micromanaging is very fine and in some cases blurry. If you want your business to operate with a level of flexibility (which is best; otherwise, you may stifle creativity), ensure that controls are in place so that work gets done.

1. Create Annual Goals

Every year, we set three to five goals that everyone in the entire company rallies behind. We ask ourselves the following question: If we looked back at the end of the year and this is all that we accomplished, would we be satisfied? At the end of the year, those are the only goals that matter.

2. Develop Quarterly Objectives

Every department leader sets objectives that stem from the annual goals we set for the company. Each department will also set department-wide objectives. The objectives are then assigned to managers within the department who are responsible for delegating and project managing throughout the course of the quarter. The managers are accountable for the objectives, and their teams are responsible for delivering on them.

In an effort to document our journey and increase transparency, I also write a quarterly letter in which I reflect on the things that went well and the things that didn't go as planned throughout the quarter. It also allows me to solicit help and anticipate what we have ahead of us for the following quarter.

3. Focus on Monthly Targets

Every month, we update a Key Performance Indicator (KPI) dashboard that is managed by the executive team. Once it is populated, we reflect on it with the company leadership team, and then I put together an email to the entire company that includes the dashboard and comments on how we are doing toward our annual goals. This creates an incredible amount of accountability and transparency within the organization. Everyone has access to this document, and they can easily see how we are managing our expenses, how much revenue we're bringing in, and what our company's burn rate is in that given moment. The executive team then holds a monthly town hall for people to bring up any questions or concerns they may have.

4. Have Weekly Emails

Toward the end of every week, we ask everyone in the organization to send a brief email to his or her manager. The email has three sections: challenges, successes, and a third section for anything the manager or company should start/stop/continue. They are meant to be short and sweet, with the purpose of really shedding light on key items.

5. Do Daily Check-ins

Every morning at 9:05 a.m. we have a group huddle. Everyone present in the office forms a circle and comes prepared to share the most significant thing that happened the day before, the most important thing (just one) that they will accomplish that day, and whether or not they foresee anything slowing them down. This usually takes us between seven and ten minutes. It also provides an opportunity to share any important company-wide announcements as they come up, instead of trying to create a meeting with a long agenda or sending a handful of emails.

Chapter Thirty-one

LEADING THROUGH A CRISIS

"I do not pray for a lighter load, but for a stronger back."
—Philips Brooks

Every decision we make says something about who we are and what we value. But what do you do when all the options you must choose between make you sick to your stomach? Is there really such a thing as a lesser of two evils?

I found myself in that very position halfway through the first week of our programs one summer at Practice Makes Perfect. In the weeks leading up to the first day of our programs, our team had enrolled kids to fill 96 percent of the potential seats we had across the city. On day one, only about 70 percent of the kids showed up. To make matters worse, the attrition was concentrated across 20 percent of our sites, meaning there were classes where my team expected fifty students and only ten were present on the first day.

Our team tried not to panic. Again, it was just the first day of the program. Maybe they would show up tomorrow. Instead of spending time reflecting on why this could be, we spent the first day making calls to the kids who did not show up. By the end of the day, we knew we were in a bad place. The kids who had not shown up were not going to show up. What we didn't realize was that many of our parents were indifferent to what programs their kids were enrolled in and simply signed them up for multiple programs that ran at the same time. Many of our families had signed up for the programs in March and April, and with very little contact from us leading up to the first day of the program, they decided on another set of plans.

We bill our schools on a per class basis. While we share in the responsibility of making sure the kids are enrolled in the programs, we take full ownership over the heavy lifting that involves hiring, onboarding, and training the staff. We delivered on our part. However, something didn't feel right about billing a school for two classes' worth of kids when they only had half of a class's worth of kids show up. To make matters worse, it cost us $25,000 per day to keep everyone on payroll during the summer. We were employing over 300 people across New York City. This was when things got tricky.

By the end of the day on Tuesday, we realized there was no way to bring the enrollment levels up at some of our partner schools, which put us in one of the toughest places we've ever been in. *Do we bill our partners the full cost of the programs even though their programs were not completely enrolled? Do we refund their money and break our promise to our staff by laying them off?*

We considered every possibility, including imagining new services we could provide to the schools to ameliorate the situation, but I couldn't stomach the idea of a bait-and-switch. If the schools decided they wanted to repurpose the funds for other services we could offer, then that would be fine. But I couldn't force them into ancillary services.

By day three, we realized there was no straightforward way out of this position. Everyone was on edge, and a decision had to be made quickly if we were going to alleviate any small part of this catastrophe.

What I didn't recognize while I was in college was that the same skill set I was using to choose between two good decisions was the same skill set I would need to rely on when I had to choose between two tough decisions. Again, I needed to understand my values and allow my values to drive my decisions.

I couldn't get over how hypocritical I would be if we kept all the staff and didn't credit or refund the schools their money. But laying off some of the seasonal help would betray the trust we had built with these individuals. Both decisions felt incredibly wrong. I learned what it felt like to have to lead in times of making tough decisions.

I made the decision that aligned most with my values. I told the team we were going to move forward with layoffs that would affect up to 10 percent of our seasonal staff. The message would be communicated before the end of the week, and I would personally deliver the news to those who were affected, and later update the entire organization. We would return almost a quarter million dollars, making us a company that I could at least be proud of when I was speaking to our school partners.

My business development manager and I reached out to our impacted partners and shared the news. Most of our partners were grateful and impressed that we would act in such a way. But there was one that was not so happy that we were going to break our promises to our seasonal staff. While it was unexpected, it reminded me that we have a responsibility to the tax payers who ultimately fund our schools.

Our teammates on the recruitment team were tasked with identifying the seasonal staff who would be least impacted by the layoffs (i.e., people who hadn't moved out of state, didn't communicate financial hardship, and weren't dependent on this experience to get their next job). We chose to ignore teaching ability because we believed if you were selected out of a pool of 1,200 applicants, you were equally qualified to help us execute on our mission. A few other people on our team were tasked with finding alternative placements at other organizations for the people who were being laid off, creating opportunities for them to volunteer with our team or with other nonprofit partners, and thinking through how we might give them preferential treatment for future internships if they were willing to trust us again. The process was far from perfect, but, in hindsight, I am incredibly proud of how our team handled the situation.

That Friday, morale was at an all-time low. Some people cried. Others made it clear they never wanted to see my guts again. I couldn't blame them. This was a breakdown in execution. Ultimately, I was responsible. People had committed themselves to our organization because of the vision I had laid out, and I let them down.

It took weeks before morale within our entire company returned to where it was right before the summer. Despite the ugly that came with the start of summer 2017, there were a lot of bright spots, including the growth our kids made and how satisfied many of our partners were. Since then, we've continued to think through safeguards, including a cash reserve to absorb such a loss without ever having to lay off another seasonal employee again and an added program guarantee that all of our classes will have a minimum of fifteen students in them. Like with all of our guarantees, we will offer participants the program the following year for half the price if we fail to deliver. This brings us one step closer to reducing the risk associated with partnering with us, to try something new, and to being a true partner who only succeeds when our partners succeed.

Hopefully, we'll never find ourselves choosing between these two poor decisions again. While we may have lost some credibility with our seasonal staff in the short run, we hope that we've modeled how all companies should act in the education space to responsibly use tax-payer dollars, regardless of nonprofit or for-profit legal structure. Unfortunately, we can't eliminate the possibility of having to choose between two equally bad decisions in the future. Next time, however, I'll be far more prepared because of my deeper understanding of why I set out to do this work and the clarity I have around my values that are at the core of how I operate.

CONCLUSION

The most important thing is having the humility to learn from your mistakes. No one is perfect. No business is perfect. And no business was built in a perfect set of conditions. Commit yourself to the mindset you need to navigate it all. So much of success or failure in business is being able to see the tools and mobilizing the resources you need in that moment to continue moving forward.

Why I Would Choose the Startup Road All Over Again

Being an entrepreneur means assuming a lot of responsibility. There are definitely more positives than negatives that make this job worthwhile. If I had the chance to go back to day one, I would make the same decision all over again to start Practice Makes Perfect.

- **You get to pick your team.**

As an entrepreneur, you can't build a startup on your own. Eventually, you will require other people, which means you have the opportunity to pick your team. Surrounding yourself with people you like is probably the most important piece of workplace satisfaction. This has been incredibly meaningful for me, because I have built my closest friendships post-graduation with the people I work with.

- **You get to build something.**

This part of the job was not very material to me a year ago. We had a name and an empty Dropbox. A year later, we have over a thousand files, a structure, a team, and a brand. There is an incredible amount of satisfaction that comes from knowing that your hard work and time has amounted to something tangible.

- **You own the relationships.**

Unless you take on a job as a relationship manager, you will be stuck doing work for people you will probably never meet or get to interact with. For some people that is fine. For me, I love meeting and interacting with people. I enjoy hearing about their stories and their journeys. This makes the work you are engaged in that much more meaningful.

- **You dictate the culture.**

Here is your chance to decide how people feel when they come to work. What are the things you want people to think about when they hear about your company? This is your opportunity to create that atmosphere. For me, culture is on the top of my mind daily. We want to make sure the smart people who have joined our team continue to find meaning, purpose, and a place within our organization.

- **You learn a lot about yourself.**

I can't overstate how important this has been for me. Yes, your twenties are supposed to be a time when you make the most transformative changes to your identity. But I think being transformative is second to running a company. If you are open to feedback and the ideas of others, you will learn a lot about who you are. I can't imagine how I lived my life not fully understanding some of the things I know about myself today.

- **You never really want to stop working.**

There will be days where you will be tired, but there will always be so much you want to do to make yourself, your team, and your company that much better. That is a never-ending reward.

There is something special about taking on a job that has no defined path: you get to chart the course and make it happen.

ABOUT THE AUTHOR

Karim is CEO of Practice Makes Perfect, a company that partners with schools to help narrow the achievement gap. He received over a quarter million dollars in scholarships to make his education possible. Karim founded PMP at 18. He is an author, a TED Fellow, and an Echoing Green Fellow.

At 23, he was named to Forbes' *30 under 30* list in Education and at 24 was named to Magic Johnson's *32 under 32* list. In 2016, he was ranked in the top 3 most powerful young entrepreneurs under 25 in the world. Karim's TED Talk was named one of the *9 Most Inspiring Talks of 2017* and his Forbes day-in-the-life feature is Forbes' second most viewed of all time, collectively garnering over 4 million views. He graduated in the top 10% of his class from Cornell University and is working on a Master's in Education Policy at Columbia University.

CPSIA information can be obtained
at www.ICGtesting.com
Printed in the USA
BVHW060541170222
629284BV00003B/6